CONTENTS

Prologue:	1
Chapter 1: Introduction to Investing: Why Every Penny Counts and How They Can Make More Pennies!	8
Chapter 2: Setting Your Investment Goals, or How to Plan Your Financial Treasure Hunt	18
Chapter 3: Starting Your Investment Journey on a Shoestring Budget	59
Chapter 4: The Mechanics of Investing: From Opening Accounts to Outsmarting Taxes	70
Chapter 5: The Art of Diversification: Or How to Not Put All Your Eggs in One Basket	78
Chapter 6: Navigating the Investment Highway	90
Chapter 7: Oops! Avoiding Common Investing Blunders	97
Chapter 8: Keeping Your Investments Fit and Fab: Monitoring and Knowing When to Say Goodbye	101
Glossary	113
Further Resources:	116

PROLOGUE:

Welcome to the Wild World of Investing!

Imagine you're in a vast jungle filled with strange and wonderful creatures—lions, tigers, and... bulls and bears? Oh, and there are some stocks and bonds fluttering around the trees too. Welcome to the wild, wild world of investing, where the flora and fauna are made up of market charts and investment opportunities!

Now, I know what you're thinking: "I don't even know what a stock really is, and now I'm supposed to dodge financial lions and ride market bulls?" Fear not, dear explorer! You've picked up the right guidebook. Whether you've got a big, overflowing chest of gold coins, or just a few crumpled bills you found under your sofa cushions, this journey is just as much for you.

Picture yourself standing at the edge of this jungle, your backpack filled with curiosity and a map that looks more like a puzzle than a guide. The trees are thick with investment jargon, the air buzzing with the hum of market trends. As you step forward, you'll encounter the majestic stock trees, with their branches reaching high into the sky, laden with fruits of potential profits. Beware, though, for the ground is also teeming with pitfalls disguised as quick gains and too-good-to-be-true schemes.

But here's the secret: you don't need to be a seasoned explorer to navigate this terrain. Think of me as your trusty guide, armed with a machete to clear the path and a magnifying glass to spot those hidden gems. Together, we'll learn to identify the tracks of the elusive dividend-yielding stocks, recognize the call of the rising market, and avoid the traps set by market predators.

As we journey deeper, you'll find that this jungle is not just a place of danger but also of immense beauty and opportunity. The streams of compound interest flow quietly, nourishing the roots of your investments. The sunlit clearings, where diversification grows in harmony, will become your safe-havens.

So, whether you're embarking on this adventure with a treasure chest of riches or just the spare change in your pocket, remember that every great explorer started with a single step. Let's take that step together and turn the wild, wild world of investing into your own personal safari of financial freedom!

This book is your simple, beginner's guide—a stepping stone to help you gain enough knowledge to start small and move forward with continuous education. Each page is a breadcrumb, leading you to greater financial understanding and the confidence to explore further. By the end, you'll be less like a financial deer in headlights and more like a savvy squirrel who knows exactly where to stash those acorns.

Who This Book Is For

This book is for anyone who's ever found themselves staring blankly at a financial news report, feeling like it's broadcasted in alien code. It's for those of you who've heard about the mystical land of "Wall Street," but wouldn't know how to get there if it was programmed into your GPS. It's especially for those who believe that investing is like an exclusive club, where only the rich and wise hold memberships.

If your bank account has never housed more than a few zeros (after a number other than zero, hopefully!), or if the term "mutual fund" makes you think of a group savings pot for mutual friends, then, my friend, you're in the right place.

This book is for the everyday person—the one who works hard, saves what they can, and dreams of a future where money worries are a thing of the past. It's for the single parent balancing bills and looking for a way to build a better future for their kids. It's for the recent college graduate, eager to make smart financial decisions but overwhelmed by the sea of information out there.

It's for the couple nearing retirement, realizing they need to make their savings stretch further, and for the young professional just starting out, wanting to make every dollar count. It's for anyone who's felt intimidated by the jargon, the charts, and the seemingly complex world of investing.

You don't need a degree in finance or a hefty bank balance to start investing. What you need is a willingness to learn, a dash of patience, and the courage to take that first step. This book breaks down complex concepts into bite-sized, digestible pieces, making the world of investing accessible to everyone.

If you've ever thought that investing was only for those with suits, ties, and a Wall Street address, think again. This book will show you that the power to grow your wealth lies within your grasp, no matter where you start from.

So whether you're just curious about the stock market or ready to dip your toes into the investment waters, this book is your gateway. Let's embark on this journey together, turning the daunting world of investing into an exciting adventure filled with opportunities for growth and financial freedom.

Why You Should Invest

FLIPS.

"But why should I invest?" you might ask. Imagine you could plant a tree in your backyard today and just by giving it a little water every now and then, you could pick money off its branches in a few years. Wouldn't you want to start planting right away? Well, investing is a lot like planting a money tree, except better, because you don't have to worry about it getting eaten by squirrels.

Investing is how you make your money work for you. It's how that tiny seed grows into a towering tree. Sure, it might seem scary now, but every expert investor was once a beginner, standing at the edge of this same jungle, deciding whether to step in.

Think of investing as sending your money on a mission to bring back reinforcements. You can either let your cash sit idly in a bank account, like a couch potato binging on TV shows, or you can send it out to work hard and multiply. Investing is like signing your dollars up for a fitness program where they get stronger and more numerous over time.

Now, you might be worried about the risks, and that's perfectly normal. Even the bravest explorers get a little jittery before embarking on an adventure. But here's the thing: not investing is also a risk. Inflation, which is basically the slow and steady increase in prices over time, can eat away at your savings like termites gnawing on wood. By investing, you give your money a fighting chance to grow and outpace inflation.

Think about your future dreams—buying a house, traveling the world, starting your own business, or retiring comfortably. Investing is the vehicle that can help you reach those dreams faster. It's like booking a first-class ticket on the express train to Financial Freedom Town, instead of hitchhiking and hoping for the best.

And don't worry, you don't need to become a financial wizard overnight. This book is here to break down the process into manageable steps. You'll learn how to water your investment tree with regular contributions and watch it grow through the magic of compound interest. Over time, you'll see that little sapling turn into a mighty oak, providing shade and shelter for your financial future.

So, put on your explorer hat and get ready to plant those seeds. With patience, knowledge, and a bit of courage, you'll transform your financial landscape into a lush, money-bearing forest.

The Journey Ahead

As your self-appointed guide on this adventure, I've trekked these trails before. I've had my fair share of slips, falls, and yes, the occasional faceplant into the mud of financial blunders. I'll share these tales not only because they're embarrassingly funny, but because there's a lot you can learn from them.

We'll start with the absolute basics—what stocks are, why bonds are not just old-fashioned agreements written on fancy paper, and why keeping all your money in a savings account is like keeping a racehorse in a tiny backyard shed. It can do so much more if you just let it run on the track!

Picture this: you're at the starting line of a grand adventure, with your trusty guide (that's me) leading the way. I'll point out the potholes and the scenic viewpoints, sharing my misadventures to help you avoid the same pitfalls. You'll learn about stocks, those little slices of a company that can grow like beanstalks if nurtured properly. We'll demystify bonds, revealing that they're not just dusty relics from your grandparents' attic, but powerful tools that can provide steady income and stability.

And then there's the savings account. Sure, it's safe and cozy, like wrapping your money in bubble wrap and placing it in a padded box. But let's be real—would you keep a racehorse in your backyard shed? Of course not! That thoroughbred needs space to run, to stretch its legs, to show off its speed. Similarly, your money needs the opportunity to grow, to compound, to multiply.

We'll journey through the dense forest of financial terms, hacking away the jargon and clearing a path to understanding. By the end, you'll be able to navigate the investment landscape with confidence, armed with knowledge and a few good laughs from my own financial faceplants.

You'll learn the art of diversification, spreading your investments across different asset classes like a chef creating a balanced, delicious meal. We'll explore the power of compound interest, which can turn your modest savings into a mighty sum over time —like a snowball rolling down a hill, gathering size and speed.

So lace up your boots, grab your map (this book), and let's embark on this exciting journey together. There will be challenges and surprises, but with each step, you'll grow more knowledgeable and more confident. And remember, even the most seasoned explorers started as beginners, taking that first brave step into the unknown.

Expect The Unexpected

Along the way, expect to encounter some jargon-jungles and acronym-animals that seem daunting at first. But with our handy "Deciphering Decoder," we'll translate those bizarre terms into plain English. Ever heard of a "bull market"? No, it's not a place where they sell bulls. Spoiler alert: it's actually good news for your investments!

And yes, there will be dangers: the siren calls of hot stock tips from your Uncle Jerry, the mirages of get-rich-quick schemes, and the ever-tempting impulse to panic-sell when the market dips. But with our trusty map of strategies and your newly acquired knowledge, you'll navigate these hazards like a pro.

Picture this: you're sailing on the ocean of investing. Occasionally, you'll hit choppy waters and stormy weather. But instead of freaking out and abandoning ship, you'll have the confidence to steer through, knowing that calmer seas lie ahead. And hey, you might even spot some dolphins—or dividends—along the way!

Of course, every good adventure has a treasure map, and investing is no different. Your treasure map includes setting goals, staying disciplined, and keeping an eye on the horizon. X marks the spot, but instead of gold doubloons, you'll find financial security and the ability to sleep soundly at night, dreaming of your growing nest egg.

And let's not forget about the cheerleaders you'll meet on this journey. Financial advisors, online resources, and even this book are here to cheer you on, provide guidance, and help you stay motivated. Think of them as your personal GPS, guiding you towards financial success and helping you avoid the potholes along the way.

So, arm yourself with knowledge, keep your sense of humor handy, and remember that investing is a marathon, not a sprint. With patience, persistence, and a sprinkle of humor, you'll be well on your way to mastering the art of investing and turning your financial dreams into reality. Happy navigating, future financial adventurer!

Investing isn't just about growing your wealth; it's about growing as a person, gaining confidence, and enjoying the ride. So, let's make it fun! There will be puns, jokes, and maybe even a cartoon character or two to help us through the tough topics.

Buckle up, get ready, and open this book with the excitement of a kid at the entrance of a theme park. We're about to embark on a rollercoaster ride to financial freedom. And remember: every great adventure starts with a single step. Or in your case, a single page turn. Welcome aboard, future investor. Let's make some money while we have some laughs. Your journey to financial freedom starts now!

CHAPTER 1: INTRODUCTION TO INVESTING: WHY EVERY PENNY COUNTS AND HOW THEY CAN MAKE MORE PENNIES!

Welcome to the Party!

Congratulations! You've just been invited to the most exclusive (and potentially lucrative) party around—the Investing Party! Now, before you dismiss this as yet another boring financial spiel, let me assure you, this is not your grandmother's tea party. This is where the magic happens, where your pennies can grow into... well, more than pennies!

Why Invest?

So, why should you invest? Well, let me put it this way: Imagine you have a magical piggy bank. Every time you put a dollar into it, the piggy bank makes that dollar work out and get stronger. Over time, that dollar can multiply into two, three, or even ten dollars! That's what investing can do—it turns your money into a mini superhero, capable of growing and bringing back more money friends!

But let's dial back the magic analogy and get to the point: Investing is essential because it's one of the most effective ways to create wealth over time. And here's the kicker—it's not just for the rich or the finance savvy. It's for everyone, including you, who found a dollar in the laundry last week.

Imagine if you left that dollar under your mattress. Sure, it's safe from the monster under the bed, but it's not doing much else. In fact, it might even get a little lonely under there. On the other hand, if you invest that dollar, it can go out into the world, make new friends, and bring them all back to you. Think of it as sending your money to a really productive party—everyone comes back with more friends, and your wealth grows!

Now, you might be thinking, "I don't have much to invest." That's okay! You don't need to be rolling in dough to start investing. Even small amounts can grow over time, thanks to the magic of compound interest. Compound interest is like a snowball rolling down a hill—it starts small, but as it rolls, it picks up more snow and gets bigger and bigger. Before you know it, you've got an avalanche of wealth!

Investing also helps you beat inflation. Inflation is like that sneaky little gremlin that slowly eats away at your money's value. If you hide your money under the mattress, the gremlin will have a feast, and your money will lose its purchasing power over time. But when you invest, you're putting your money to work, potentially earning returns that outpace inflation. It's like giving that gremlin a run for its money!

Let's talk about freedom. Investing can provide financial freedom. Imagine being able to do what you want, when you want, without worrying about the next paycheck. Investing is a way to build a safety net, a cushion that can help you achieve your dreams. Whether it's buying a house, starting a business, or traveling the world, investing can help make those dreams a reality.

And here's another thing: Investing is a great way to learn and grow. It's like a never-ending adventure with twists and turns, ups and downs. You learn about different companies, industries, and markets. You become more knowledgeable and savvy, and who knows, you might even find it fun! Yes, fun! It's like a game where you're constantly learning new strategies and improving your skills. And the best part? You get to watch your wealth grow along the way.

But wait, there's more! Investing can also be a way to support causes you care about. There are investment options that focus on sustainability, social responsibility, and ethical practices. So, not only can you grow your wealth, but you can also make a positive impact on the world. It's like being a financial superhero, fighting for the greater good while building your nest egg.

Let's not forget about retirement. Investing is crucial for building a comfortable retirement. We all want to enjoy our golden years, right? Imagine sipping a piña colada on a beach, knowing that your investments are working hard to support your lifestyle. Investing can help ensure that you have enough money to live comfortably when you decide to hang up your work boots and retire.

Investing is like giving your money a purpose, a mission to grow and multiply. It's not about getting rich quick or gambling away your hard-earned cash. It's about making smart decisions, being patient, and letting time work its magic. Whether you're investing a little or a lot, the key is to start. So, take that dollar you found in the laundry, give it a mission, and watch as it transforms into something much greater. Happy investing!

A Little Goes A Long Way

Think you need big bucks to start investing? Think again! Thanks to modern technology and some nifty financial tools, you can start investing with just a few bucks. Yes, even the amount you might spend on a coffee can now be turned into an investment. Instead of watching your coffee disappear sip by sip, you could watch your money grow day by day. Which cup would you choose?

Now, I know what you're thinking: "But I love my daily coffee!" And who doesn't? But imagine this: Instead of buying that extra-large caramel macchiato with whipped cream and sprinkles, you invest that money. Sure, you'll miss out on a few moments of caffeinated bliss, but in the long run, your future self will thank you. Picture this: Future You, lounging on a beach, sipping a piña colada, funded by the dollars you didn't spend on those coffees. Sweet deal, right?

Another great thing about starting small is that it's less scary. You don't need to be a Wall Street wizard to invest a few bucks. Think of it as dipping your toes into the pool before diving in. You get to learn the ropes, understand how investing works, and build your confidence. Before you know it, you'll be doing cannonballs into the deep end of the investing pool!

And let's be honest, watching your money grow is way more exciting than watching your coffee cup empty. It's like having a pet plant that thrives on its own without you needing to water it every day. You get to see those small investments sprout, grow leaves, and eventually blossom into a beautiful money tree. No green thumb required!

Plus, investing small amounts can help you build good habits. It's like training for a marathon. You don't start by running 26 miles on day one. You start with a mile, then two, then three, until you're ready for the big race. Investing works the same way. Start small, stay consistent, and over time, you'll build the financial stamina to tackle bigger goals.

And here's a fun thought: Imagine telling your friends that you're an investor. It has a nice ring to it, doesn't it? You don't have to mention that you started with the cost of a latte. What matters is that you're taking steps to secure your financial future. You're in the game, and that's something to be proud of.

So, next time you're tempted to splurge on something you don't really need, think about how that money could be invested instead. It might seem like a small sacrifice now, but those small sacrifices can add up to something big. Investing is like planting a garden. You start with seeds, and with a little patience and care, you end up with a bounty of fruits and vegetables. Or in this case, dollars and cents.

Remember, it's not about how much you start with; it's about starting. So go ahead, take that first step. Your future self will raise a glass (or a coffee cup) to your wise decision. Cheers to investing!

The Early Bird Gets The Wealth

Starting early is like getting a VIP pass to this party. The earlier you start, the more your money can work its magic. It's not just about saving money; it's about giving your money enough time to dance on the financial dance floor and multiply.

Let's break it down: If you start investing at 20 years old rather than 30, you give your money an extra decade to grow. This doesn't mean you're late if you start at 30, 40, or even 50, but like in any party, the earlier you arrive, the more appetizers (or in this case, returns) you get to enjoy.

Think of investing early as being the first to arrive at an all-you-can-eat buffet. You get the freshest, hottest, and tastiest dishes before anyone else. By the time the latecomers arrive, you're already on your second plate, savoring the delicious returns while they're just figuring out where the line starts.

Now, picture this: you're a 20-year-old and decide to invest the cost of one pizza a month. Not only are you saving yourself from the extra calories, but you're also setting yourself up for a financial feast in the future. By the time you're 30, that pizza money has invited its friends and thrown a wealth party in your investment account.

Starting early also means you get to learn and make mistakes while you're young. It's like trying out new dance moves at the beginning of the night. If you trip or stumble, no big deal! You've got the whole night to perfect your groove. Similarly, early investing lets you ride out the ups and downs of the market with time on your side.

Plus, early investing is like planting a tree. The sooner you plant it, the more time it has to grow tall and strong, providing shade (and money) for years to come. Imagine sitting under that tree, enjoying the fruits of your early investment efforts, while others are still trying to figure out where to buy seeds.

So, whether you're 20 or 50, remember: the best time to start investing was yesterday, but the second best time is today. Grab your VIP pass, hit the financial dance floor, and let your money show off its best moves. The sooner you start, the sooner you'll be enjoying the wealth party you've created!

But Isn't Investing Risky?

Sure, investing comes with its risks—there's no denying it. But here's a fun fact: Not investing is risky too! Inflation is like the party pooper that slowly eats away the value of your money. By not investing, you might be losing money without even spending it. Sounds like a bad deal, right?

Now, I'm not saying you should throw all your savings into

the next hot stock your cousin Vinny mentioned at the family BBQ. Instead, I'm talking about calculated, informed investing—putting your money in places where it has a good chance to grow while still letting you sleep at night.

Imagine your money as a bunch of couch potatoes. If they just sit around doing nothing, they'll eventually wither away thanks to the sneaky thief called inflation. But if you send them to the financial gym (a.k.a. investing), they'll get stronger and healthier, ready to take on the world.

Think of investing like cooking a gourmet meal. You wouldn't just toss random ingredients into a pot and hope for the best (unless you're on a reality cooking show, and even then, it's risky). You follow a recipe, measure carefully, and taste along the way. Similarly, informed investing means doing your homework, understanding what you're getting into, and making adjustments as needed.

Let's face it: life is full of risks. Driving a car, eating sushi from that new place around the corner, or trusting your friend's advice on hairstyles—all come with their own set of risks. But we don't let that stop us, do we? We just try to make smart choices, like wearing a seatbelt, checking Yelp reviews, or maybe double-checking that hairstyle recommendation.

When it comes to investing, think of risk like a spice. A little bit can add excitement and flavor, but too much can set your mouth on fire. The key is finding the right balance. Diversify your investments, spread out the risk, and don't put all your eggs in one basket (or all your dollars in one stock). This way, even if one investment goes sour, the others can help balance things out.

And remember, you don't have to go it alone. Financial advisors, robo-advisors, and a plethora of online resources are like your financial sous-chefs, helping you navigate the complexities of investing without breaking a sweat.

So yes, investing has its risks, but with a little knowledge, some strategic planning, and consistency, you can turn those risks into rewards. After all, the biggest risk might be not taking any risk at all.

A World Of Opportunities

Investing opens up a world of opportunities. It's like having a ticket to every concert on the planet. Want to own a piece of a tech giant or a start-up that's about to revolutionize the world? You can! Interested in real estate but can't buy an entire building? Real estate investment trusts (REITs) have got you covered. There are so many ways to invest, from stocks and bonds to mutual funds and beyond.

And the best part? You don't need to be an expert. With robo-advisors and online platforms, the investing world has never been more accessible. These tools do most of the heavy lifting, so you don't need to quit your day job and become a Wall Street wizard.

Think of robo-advisors as your financial personal trainers. They create a customized workout plan for your money and make sure it stays on track. Meanwhile, you can sit back, relax, and occasionally check in to see those financial muscles growing. It's like having a money-making robot butler!

The variety of investment options means there's something for everyone. It's like a buffet with endless choices. Whether you're into tech, green energy, or just want something low-risk, there's an investment option that fits your taste. You can mix and match, creating a diversified portfolio that reflects your interests and risk tolerance.

And let's not forget about the thrill of being part of something bigger. When you invest, you're not just making money; you're helping companies grow, supporting innovation, and contributing to the economy. It's like being a backstage VIP at the concert of economic progress.

So, grab your ticket, explore the buffet, and let the robo-advisors handle the heavy lifting. The world of investing is vast and exciting, and it's waiting for you to dive in. Happy investing!

It's A Learning Curve

Investing is also a fantastic way to learn. Each investment is a lesson in economics, business, psychology, and so much more. You'll start to understand the "why" behind market ups and downs, get a feel for trends, and maybe even discover a thing or two about your own risk tolerance.

Think of investing as enrolling in the school of life. Instead of textbooks, you have real-world experiences. You'll learn why certain companies thrive and others don't, how global events impact markets, and what makes investors tick. It's like getting a front-row seat to the world's biggest and most exciting classroom.

And the best part? The lessons you learn from investing aren't just for the stock market—they apply to everyday life. You'll develop better decision-making skills, learn to manage uncertainty, and gain confidence in handling your finances. It's like building a toolkit that helps you navigate both your financial future and your personal life.

Don't worry if it feels overwhelming at first. Just like learning to ride a bike, you might wobble a bit, but with practice, you'll find your balance. And who knows? You might even start enjoying the ride. So buckle up, embrace the learning curve, and get ready to grow not just your wealth, but also your knowledge and confidence.

Let's Get This Party Started!

So, are you ready to get this party started? Grab your metaphorical party hat (a.k.a. your investor cap), throw in your first few dollars, and let's watch them grow. Remember, investing isn't just for the old and wealthy; it's for everyone looking to make their financial future brighter. And who knows? You might just have some fun along the way. After all, money might not grow on trees, but it can definitely grow in your investment account!

Think of your investment journey as the ultimate adventure. There will be highs, lows, and everything in between, but each step brings you closer to your financial goals. You're not just a bystander—you're an active participant in your financial destiny. So, put on your dancing shoes, embrace the excitement, and get ready to celebrate your financial wins. Here's to making smart investments, learning along the way, and building a brighter, more secure future. Let's get this investment party started!

Welcome aboard!

CHAPTER 2: SETTING YOUR INVESTMENT GOALS, OR HOW TO PLAN YOUR FINANCIAL TREASURE HUNT

Welcome To The Game Of Goals

Investing without a goal is like going on a treasure hunt without a map. Sure, wandering can be fun, but wouldn't you rather find the treasure? In this chapter, we're going to sketch out your treasure map. We'll figure out whether you're hunting for quick golden nuggets or the legendary Lost City of Gold. In other words, are we setting short-term goals or eyeing long-term riches?

First things first, let's talk about why goals are important. Having clear investment goals gives you direction and purpose. It's like setting your GPS before a road trip—you know where you're headed and how to get there. Without goals, you might end up driving in circles, wasting time and energy.

Short-term goals are like grabbing those shiny golden nuggets. These are goals you want to achieve in the next few years, like saving for a vacation, a new gadget, or building an emergency fund. They're exciting and give you a taste of what investing can do for you. Short-term goals keep you motivated and show you the immediate benefits of investing.

On the other hand, long-term goals are like the legendary Lost City of Gold. These are the big, life-changing goals that take time and patience to achieve, like buying a house, funding your children's education, or retiring comfortably. Long-term goals require a bit more strategy and discipline, but the rewards are worth it. They provide financial security and the freedom to live the life you've always dreamed of.

To get started, think about what you want to achieve. Write down your goals, no matter how big or small. Be specific—how much money do you need, and by when? This clarity will help you stay focused and measure your progress along the way.

Next, prioritize your goals. Which ones are the most important to you? Which ones can wait? Prioritizing helps you allocate your resources effectively and make informed decisions about where to invest your money.

Remember, goals can change. Life happens, and your priorities might shift. That's okay! The key is to be flexible and adjust your map as needed. Your treasure might move, but as long as you keep your eyes on the prize, you'll find your way.

So, welcome to the game of goals. Let's sketch out your map, set your sights on your treasure, and embark on this exciting journey together. With clear goals and a solid plan, you're well on your way to finding your financial treasure. Let the adventure begin!

The Tale of Two Treasures: Short-term vs. Long-term Goals

Short-Term Goals: Sprinting To Success

Imagine this: you've got your eye on the latest gaming console, a top-of-the-line blender that could whip up a storm, or perhaps you're planning the ultimate Halloween party that will have the whole neighborhood talking for years. These aren't dreams for some distant future; they're right around the corner. That's what short-term goals are all about—usually one to three years away. It's like gearing up for a sprint rather than a marathon. You want results fast, like microwave popcorn—quick, satisfying, and oh-so-gratifying.

Short-term goals are the little bursts of excitement that keep you motivated. They're the quick wins that make you feel accomplished and ready to take on the next challenge. To achieve these, you'll need to focus on investments that offer more immediate returns. Think of them as the hare in our investment jungle—fast, energetic, and always on the move.

Where To Stash The Cash?

When you're aiming for these quick wins, you don't want to play too risky. After all, losing your savings for that Halloween bash would be a horror story in itself! So, where do you park your cash to make sure it's both safe and accessible? Let's dive into some smart, safe spots that are the savings equivalents of keeping your socks in a drawer—secure, easy to access, and straightforward.

Think of these places as your financial safety nets. They're not about making a fortune overnight, but about keeping your money secure while still allowing it to grow a bit. It's like finding a cozy spot in your home where you know your valuables are protected, but you can also grab them quickly when you need them.

First, there are savings accounts. They might not offer the thrill of high returns, but they give you peace of mind, knowing your money is just a click away whenever you need it. It's like having a trusty piggy bank, except this one might give you a tiny bit of interest in return for storing your cash.

Then there are certificates of deposit (CDs). These are like the lockboxes of the financial world—you put your money in, lock it away for a set period, and earn a bit more interest in return. Just be prepared to leave it alone for a while, like keeping a secret stash hidden until the perfect moment to reveal it.

Money market accounts are another good option. They offer a bit more flexibility and often higher interest rates than regular savings accounts, with the added bonus of being just as accessible. Imagine them as your emergency fund's best friend—reliable, flexible, and ready to help out when needed.

So, when thinking about where to stash your cash for short-term goals, prioritize safety and accessibility. You want to ensure your money is there when you need it, without the stress of high risks. By choosing the right spots, you can sleep easy knowing your Halloween bash or that shiny new gadget is just around the corner, waiting to be enjoyed.

High-Yield Savings Accounts: The No-Fuss Saver

Think of high-yield savings accounts as your financial best friend who always has your back. These accounts offer higher interest rates compared to regular savings accounts, meaning your money grows faster without you lifting a finger. They're like a turbo boost for your savings, helping you reach your short-term goals quicker. Plus, they're super accessible. Need to pull out some cash for an unexpected expense? No problem—your money is just a click away.

Imagine having a best friend who's always looking out for your financial well-being, making sure your money isn't just sitting around lazily but actually doing some work. High-yield savings accounts are that friend, giving your savings a little extra oomph without any extra effort on your part.

These accounts are the financial equivalent of a no-fuss, reliable sidekick. You deposit your money, sit back, and watch it grow a bit faster than it would in a regular savings account. It's like having a plant that not only survives but thrives with minimal care—just the occasional watering (or deposit), and it's flourishing.

What's even better is the accessibility. High-yield savings accounts are designed to be user-friendly and straightforward. If an unexpected expense pops up, like a surprise vet bill for your adventurous cat or an emergency repair for your trusty car, you can easily transfer money from your high-yield savings account. It's like having a safety net that's both cushy and within arm's reach.

So, if you're looking for a place to park your money where it can grow steadily and remain easily accessible, high-yield savings accounts are the way to go. They combine the security of a savings account with the added benefit of higher interest rates, making them an ideal choice for short-term goals. It's the ultimate blend of convenience and growth, ensuring your financial journey is smooth and rewarding.

Money Market Accounts: The Flexible Friend

Next up, we have money market accounts. These are a bit like high-yield savings accounts but with a twist. They often come with check-writing privileges and debit cards, giving you the flexibility to access your funds in multiple ways. It's like having a savings account that moonlights as a checking account. You get the best of both worlds—higher interest rates and the convenience of easy access to your money. It's perfect for those short-term goals where you might need to dip into your savings now and then.

Think of money market accounts as your flexible friend who's always ready for any situation. Need to write a check for that last-minute payment? No problem. Want to swipe a debit card for an unexpected purchase? Easy peasy. These accounts give you the freedom to manage your money without the usual constraints of traditional savings accounts.

Imagine your money market account as a versatile tool in your financial toolkit. It combines the steady growth of a savings account with the practical features of a checking account. It's like having a Swiss Army knife for your finances—ready to tackle any financial need that comes your way.

Money market accounts offer the added bonus of higher interest rates, so your savings grow faster than they would in a regular savings account. It's like having a garden where the plants grow a bit taller and stronger with each passing day, all while being able to pick a fresh flower whenever you need one.

The flexibility of money market accounts makes them ideal for short-term goals. Whether you're saving for a big-ticket item or just need a reliable place to park your emergency fund, these accounts provide the perfect balance of growth and accessibility. You can easily dip into your savings when needed, without the hassle of moving money around.

So, if you're looking for a smart, flexible way to manage your short-term savings, money market accounts are the way to go. They give you the best of both worlds—higher returns on your savings and the convenience of easy access to your funds. It's the perfect combination for anyone who wants to keep their financial options open while still growing their money.

Certificates Of Deposit (Cds): The Safe Keeper

If you're more of a set-it-and-forget-it type, certificates of deposit (CDs) might be your jam. Think of CDs as a financial time capsule. You deposit your money, lock it away for a set period (anywhere from a few months to several years), and when the time is up, you get your money back with interest. CDs usually offer higher interest rates than regular savings accounts because you're committing to leave your money untouched for a while. It's a great option if you have a specific timeline for your goal and don't need immediate access to your funds.

Imagine you're creating a financial time capsule. You carefully place your money inside, seal it up, and set a date in the future to open it. Over time, your money isn't just sitting idle—it's growing with interest, ready to be unveiled at just the right moment. That's the magic of CDs.

Think of CDs as your reliable, no-nonsense safe keeper. Once you've made your deposit, you can forget about it, knowing that it's securely locked away and earning interest. It's like putting your savings on autopilot—no need for constant check-ins or adjustments. When the term ends, you get back your initial deposit plus a nice chunk of interest, making it a rewarding surprise.

The key to CDs is commitment. By agreeing to leave your money untouched for a specified period, you earn higher interest rates compared to regular savings accounts. It's like committing to a long-term fitness plan—stick with it, and you'll see impressive results over time.

CDs are perfect for those goals with a clear timeline. Planning a big purchase in a couple of years? Saving for a wedding or a dream vacation? CDs provide a structured way to grow your savings without the temptation of dipping into them prematurely. They're the financial equivalent of setting a goal and steadily working towards it, confident that your efforts will pay off when the time comes.

So, if you're looking for a safe, hands-off way to grow your savings and you don't need immediate access to your funds, CDs are a fantastic option. They offer the stability and growth potential you need, wrapped up in a straightforward package. Just set it, forget it, and look forward to the day when your financial time capsule unlocks with added interest.

Balancing Safety And Growth

The key to sprinting towards your short-term goals is finding the right balance between safety and growth. You want your money to grow, but you also want to ensure it's there when you need it. High-yield savings accounts, money market accounts, and CDs provide that balance. They offer better interest rates than stuffing your cash under a mattress (or a low-yield savings account) but without the risk of losing your hard-earned money in the stock market.

Imagine you're tightrope walking between two skyscrapers. On one side is safety, and on the other is growth. You need to keep your balance to make it across without falling into financial peril. High-yield savings accounts, money market accounts, and CDs are your safety net and balance pole, giving you the confidence to stride forward without fear.

High-yield savings accounts are like your reliable gym buddy. They help you build your financial muscles steadily without the risk of injury. You get higher interest rates than a regular savings account, meaning your money grows faster while still being easily accessible.

Money market accounts are the versatile tool in your financial toolkit. They offer higher interest rates and come with check-writing privileges and debit cards, giving you the flexibility to access your funds whenever you need them. It's like having a Swiss Army knife for your finances, always ready to handle whatever comes your way.

Certificates of deposit (CDs) are your disciplined, long-term planner. They require you to lock your money away for a set period, offering higher interest rates in return. It's like planting a seed and watching it grow into a sturdy tree over time, knowing you'll reap the benefits when the term ends.

Balancing safety and growth means choosing these smart, secure options to park your cash. They provide better interest rates than hiding your money under a mattress or in a low-yield savings account. This way, your money isn't just safe—it's actively working for you, growing steadily while being ready when you need it.

So, when you're aiming for those short-term goals, remember to find that sweet spot between safety and growth. With high-yield savings accounts, money market accounts, and CDs, you can confidently sprint towards your dreams, knowing your money is both protected and growing. It's the perfect blend of security and progress, ensuring your financial journey is smooth and rewarding.

Track Your Progress: Keep The Motivation High

There's nothing more satisfying than watching your savings grow. Use a savings app or a simple spreadsheet to track your progress. Set mini-milestones along the way and celebrate each one. Saving for that gaming console? Reward yourself with a small treat when you've saved up half the amount. Planning a Halloween bash? Maybe buy a few decorations as you reach each savings milestone. Keeping track of your progress not only keeps you motivated but also makes the journey towards your goal a lot more fun.

Imagine your savings journey as a thrilling adventure game. Each time you save, you're leveling up, getting closer to your ultimate prize. A savings app or spreadsheet is your game map, showing you where you are and how far you've come. It's like having a treasure map with X marking the spot—each deposit brings you one step closer to uncovering the treasure.

Setting mini-milestones along the way is like placing checkpoints in your game. These are little victories to celebrate and keep you motivated. Saving for that latest gaming console? When you hit the halfway mark, reward yourself with a small treat, like a favorite snack or a fun outing. Planning an epic Halloween bash? Buy a few spooky decorations each time you reach a savings milestone. These mini-rewards are like power-ups that keep you energized and excited about your progress.

Tracking your progress isn't just practical—it's a way to make saving enjoyable. Watching your savings grow is like seeing your character gain strength and abilities in a game. It's satisfying and encourages you to keep going. Plus, by celebrating each milestone, you're making the journey itself fun and rewarding, not just the end goal.

Think of your savings app or spreadsheet as your personal cheerleader. Every time you update it, you get a visual reminder of how well you're doing. It's like having a friend who constantly reminds you of your achievements and motivates you to keep pushing forward.

So, keep track of your progress and enjoy the journey. Celebrate each mini-milestone with a little treat, and let your growing savings inspire you to reach your ultimate goal. With every deposit, you're getting closer to your dream, making the process not only effective but also a lot more fun.

Stay Flexible And Adapt

Life can throw curveballs, and sometimes your savings goals might need to change. Maybe a surprise expense comes up, or you find something even more exciting to save for. Stay flexible and be willing to adapt your plan. The beauty of short-term goals is that they're just that—short-term. You can reassess and realign your goals without too much hassle.

Imagine you're on a road trip. You've planned your route and packed your bags, but suddenly you see a detour sign or discover a hidden gem that wasn't on your original map. Flexibility is key. Being willing to change your plans can lead to unexpected adventures and even better outcomes.

Staying flexible with your savings goals is like being a skilled navigator. You know your ultimate destination, but you're ready to take a different path if needed. Maybe an unexpected expense pops up, like a medical bill or car repair. Instead of panicking, you reassess your savings plan and make adjustments, just like rerouting on a road trip.

Sometimes, life presents new opportunities that are too exciting to pass up. Perhaps you were saving for a new phone, but then you discover an amazing travel deal or a course you've always wanted to take. Flexibility allows you to shift your focus and redirect your funds without feeling like you've failed. It's like finding a scenic route that's even more enjoyable than the one you initially planned.

The beauty of short-term goals is their adaptability. Unlike long-term goals, which require more commitment and planning, short-term goals can be tweaked and adjusted with relative ease. It's like having a menu of options—you can mix and match based on what's happening in your life right now.

Staying flexible also means being kind to yourself when things don't go as planned. If you need to dip into your savings for an emergency or change your goal altogether, it's okay. The key is to reassess, realign, and keep moving forward. Life is unpredictable, and your savings plan should be able to bend and stretch with it.

So, embrace flexibility and be ready to adapt. Reassess your goals regularly and make adjustments as needed. By staying open to change, you can navigate life's curveballs with confidence, ensuring your financial journey remains smooth and rewarding, no matter what comes your way.

Celebrate Your Success

When you finally hit that savings goal, make sure to celebrate! You've worked hard, been disciplined, and now it's time to reap the rewards. Whether it's unboxing that shiny new gaming console, blending up a storm with your new kitchen gadget, or throwing the Halloween party of the decade, take a moment to enjoy your success. You've earned it!

Short-term savings goals are like little sprints in the marathon of life. They're exciting, achievable, and immensely satisfying. By choosing the right savings vehicle—whether it's a high-yield savings account, a money market account, or a CD—you can ensure your money is growing safely and steadily. Automate your savings, track your progress, stay flexible, and most importantly, celebrate your successes along the way. You've got this!

Long-Term Goals: The Marathon To Millions

Now, let's say you're dreaming bigger. Maybe you want to buy a house, save for a child's college fund, or stash away enough cash to retire on a private island. These goals are more like a marathon—a long, rewarding journey that takes persistence and vision.

Investing For The Future

When it comes to long-term goals, you can afford to be bolder. Think of stocks, mutual funds, real estate, and retirement accounts like IRAs or 401(k)s as your best friends. They're like planting an oak tree. It takes time to grow, but one day it's going to be huge and strong, offering shade (or in this case, a hefty financial cushion).

Imagine your long-term investments as planting a tiny acorn in the ground. At first, it might seem insignificant, just a small seed buried in the dirt. But with time, patience, and a bit of nurturing, that acorn transforms into a mighty oak tree, providing shelter and stability. Long-term investing works the same way—you start with modest contributions, and over time, they grow into a substantial financial foundation.

Stocks are like the branches of your investment tree, reaching high and capturing the sunlight. They offer the potential for significant growth, but they can also be a bit volatile. However, with a long-term perspective, you can weather the market's ups and downs, allowing your investments to grow robustly over time.

Mutual funds are like a bundle of saplings planted together, each representing a different type of investment. This diversification helps spread risk and ensures that even if one sapling doesn't thrive, the others will keep growing, contributing to the overall strength of your investment forest.

Real estate investments are akin to sturdy tree trunks. They provide solid, tangible value and can appreciate significantly over time. Investing in property might take more initial effort and resources, but the rewards can be substantial, offering both steady income and long-term appreciation.

Retirement accounts like IRAs and 401(k)s are the roots of your financial tree, anchoring your future stability. These accounts benefit from tax advantages and compound growth, making them essential components of a long-term investment strategy. Contributing to these accounts regularly is like watering your tree, ensuring it stays healthy and continues to grow year after year.

The key to successful long-term investing is patience and consistency. Just like an oak tree doesn't grow overnight, your investments need time to mature. The magic of compound interest works best when given years, even decades, to accumulate. By starting early and contributing regularly, you give your financial tree the best chance to grow tall and strong.

So, embrace the journey of long-term investing. Be bold, plant those financial seeds, and nurture them over time. Your future self will thank you when you're enjoying the shade of your well-grown investment oak tree, with a hefty financial cushion providing comfort and security.

Stocks: The High-Risk, High-Reward Player

Stocks are like the thrill-seekers of the investment world. They can be volatile and unpredictable, but they also offer some of the highest potential returns. When you buy a stock, you're essentially buying a piece of a company. If the company does well, so do you. It's like betting on your favorite sports team and watching them win the championship. Of course, there's always a risk they might not do so well, which is why it's crucial to diversify—spread your investments across different companies and industries to minimize risk.

Imagine stocks as the daredevils of your investment portfolio. They're the skydivers, bungee jumpers, and extreme sports enthusiasts—full of excitement, potential, and a bit of unpredictability. When you invest in stocks, you're strapping in for a thrilling ride, where the highs can be exhilarating, and the lows can be stomach-churning.

Buying a stock is like owning a share of your favorite team. You're not just a spectator; you have a stake in their performance. When the team wins the championship, you share in the glory (and the financial rewards). However, just like in sports, not every season ends with a trophy. Companies can face challenges, and stock prices can fluctuate wildly. This volatility is part of the game.

But fear not, savvy investor! The key to navigating the high-flying world of stocks is diversification. Think of it as spreading your bets across multiple teams and sports. By investing in a variety of companies and industries, you reduce the risk of any single investment tanking your entire portfolio. It's like having a well-rounded sports portfolio, where a bad season in football might be offset by a winning streak in basketball or baseball.

Diversification is your safety harness in the stock market rollercoaster. It ensures that while some stocks might dip, others could soar, balancing out your overall returns. This strategy helps you manage risk and enjoy the potential high rewards that stocks can offer without losing your shirt in the process.

So, embrace stocks as the high-risk, high-reward players in your investment lineup. They bring excitement and potential for substantial growth to your portfolio. Just remember to diversify, keeping your investments spread out to minimize risk and maximize your chances of success. With a balanced approach, you can enjoy the thrill of the ride while building a strong, resilient financial future.

Mutual Funds: The Team Player

If individual stocks are like solo athletes, mutual funds are like a well-coordinated team. These funds pool money from many investors to buy a diversified portfolio of stocks, bonds, or other securities. It's like having a financial advisor who spreads your money across various investments to reduce risk. You get the benefit of diversification without having to pick and choose individual investments yourself. Plus, mutual funds are managed by professional fund managers who do the heavy lifting for you.

Imagine mutual funds as the ultimate team sport in the investment world. While individual stocks are like solo athletes, each performing their own stunts, mutual funds bring together a whole squad of financial instruments working in harmony. They pool money from a group of investors to create a diversified portfolio, much like a coach assembling a dream team of players with different skills and strengths.

Investing in a mutual fund is like having a skilled coach and team behind you. Instead of picking and managing individual investments yourself, you have professional fund managers who handle all the heavy lifting. These managers are like the experienced coaches who strategize, make plays, and ensure the team performs at its best. They spread your money across a variety of stocks, bonds, and other securities, reducing the risk of any single investment dragging down your entire portfolio.

Think of it as joining a top-tier sports team where everyone has a specific role. The stocks in the fund might be your star forwards, aiming for high growth. Bonds could be your reliable defenders, providing stability and income. Other securities might be your versatile midfielders, balancing risk and reward. Together, they create a cohesive unit that's more resilient and robust than any single player.

The beauty of mutual funds lies in their built-in diversification. By investing in a broad range of assets, they help smooth out the bumps and bruises that come with market fluctuations. It's like having a well-rounded team that can weather different seasons, ensuring consistent performance regardless of individual ups and downs.

Plus, mutual funds offer convenience and peace of mind. You don't need to be a financial expert to benefit from them. The fund managers handle the day-to-day decisions, leaving you free to enjoy the rewards of your investment without the stress of constant monitoring and adjustments. It's like being a fan in the stands, cheering for your team while the pros play the game.

So, if you're looking for a balanced, professionally managed approach to investing, mutual funds are the way to go. They provide the benefits of diversification and expert management, making your investment journey smoother and more enjoyable. With mutual funds, you're part of a winning team, working together to achieve financial success.

Real Estate: The Tangible Asset

Real estate is a favorite for many long-term investors because it offers both stability and growth potential. Buying property is like owning a piece of the earth, a tangible asset you can see and touch. Over time, property values tend to increase, providing a solid return on investment. Plus, you can earn rental income if you choose to lease your property. Think of it as planting a money tree in your backyard that not only grows but also gives you fruit every season.

Imagine real estate as your very own piece of the world. It's like owning a slice of the pie that you can walk on, build on, and enjoy. Unlike other investments, real estate is something tangible —you can visit your property, touch the walls, and feel the ground beneath your feet. It's this tangibility that makes real estate a favorite among long-term investors looking for both stability and growth.

Over time, property values tend to appreciate, much like how a well-tended garden flourishes. This appreciation can lead to substantial returns on your initial investment. Plus, if you decide to rent out your property, it's like having a money tree in your backyard that not only grows in value but also produces rental income. Each rent check is like picking fresh fruit from your financial tree, providing regular income while your investment continues to grow.

For those who find buying an entire property out of reach, there's a delicious alternative: Real Estate Investment Trusts (REITs). Think of REITs as large-scale property owners who invite you to enjoy a slice of their real estate pie. These companies own, operate, or finance income-producing properties across various sectors, from shopping malls to office buildings to apartment complexes.

Investing in a REIT allows you to partake in the real estate market without the hassle of buying, managing, or financing properties yourself. It's like being a shareholder in a vast portfolio of properties, earning a share of the income they produce. You get the benefits of real estate investment—such as potential appreciation and rental income—without having to deal with tenants, repairs, or property taxes directly.

REITs offer a way to diversify your investment portfolio with real estate, providing stability and potential growth similar to owning physical property. It's like enjoying the fruits of a large orchard without having to plant and care for each tree yourself. You simply invest, sit back, and watch your share of the income roll in.

So, whether you're buying a piece of land, a cozy home, or investing in a REIT, real estate offers a tangible, reliable way to grow your wealth. It's a solid foundation for your financial future, providing both stability and growth potential. With real estate, you're planting a money tree that can provide returns season after season, helping you build a secure and prosperous future.

The Bond Bandwagon: Rock-Solid Returns For The Long Haul

Imagine your investment portfolio is a rock band, and each type of investment is a different instrument. Stocks are your electric guitars, bringing high energy and excitement but sometimes hitting a sour note. Real estate is the steady bass, keeping the rhythm with its solid returns and tangible presence. And then, we have bonds – the reliable drummer in the back, keeping the beat steady and the band together no matter what.

Bonds are essentially IOUs issued by governments or corporations looking to raise some cash. When you buy a bond, you're lending your money to the issuer in exchange for periodic interest payments. Think of it as you becoming a VIP member of the lending club, where your money works backstage to keep the show running smoothly. The best part? When the bond matures, you get your original investment back – talk about a guaranteed encore!

Now, you might be thinking, "Bonds sound kind of...boring." But here's the twist: while they might not have the wild solos of stocks or the cool vibe of real estate, bonds are the unsung heroes that can stabilize your portfolio during the market's chaotic jam sessions. They offer a predictable income stream and lower risk, making them perfect for investors who prefer a smooth and steady performance. So, don't underestimate the drummer – bonds can keep your investment band in harmony and ensure your financial concert is a hit!

Retirement Accounts: The Long-Game Strategist

Retirement accounts like IRAs and 401(k)s are specifically designed to help you save for your golden years. These accounts offer tax advantages that can help your savings grow faster. It's like having a secret weapon in your financial arsenal. Contributions to a traditional IRA or 401(k) are typically tax-deductible, meaning you pay less in taxes now, and your investments grow tax-deferred until you withdraw them in retirement. Roth IRAs and Roth 401(k)s, on the other hand, are funded with after-tax dollars, but your withdrawals in retirement are tax-free. It's a game of strategy, deciding which type works best for your financial situation.

Imagine retirement accounts as your financial chess pieces, strategically placed to secure your future. These accounts are designed with one goal in mind: to ensure you have enough money to live comfortably during your golden years. They come with unique tax advantages, making them powerful tools in your investment strategy.

Contributing to a traditional IRA or 401(k) is like deploying a powerful knight in your financial game. These contributions are typically tax-deductible, meaning you get a tax break now, reducing your taxable income. Your investments then grow tax-deferred, which is like having your knight shielded from attacks. You only pay taxes when you withdraw the money in retirement, hopefully when you're in a lower tax bracket.

On the other side of the board, Roth IRAs and Roth 401(k)s are your stealthy bishops. You fund these accounts with after-tax dollars, so there's no immediate tax benefit. However, the real magic happens when you retire. Withdrawals from Roth accounts are tax-free, allowing you to enjoy your savings without worrying about taxes eating into your nest egg. It's like your bishop moving freely across the board, unchallenged by tax liabilities.

Choosing between traditional and Roth accounts is a strategic decision, much like deciding which piece to move in a critical chess match. Your choice depends on your current financial situation and future tax expectations. If you expect to be in a higher tax bracket in retirement, a Roth account might be the way to go. If you're looking to reduce your taxable income now, a traditional account could be more beneficial.

Retirement accounts are the epitome of long-term planning. They require patience and foresight, much like a grandmaster plotting several moves ahead. By consistently contributing to these accounts, you're building a robust financial future, ensuring that you can enjoy your retirement years without financial stress.

So, embrace retirement accounts as your long-game strategists. Whether you choose traditional or Roth, these accounts offer valuable tax advantages and a solid foundation for your retirement savings. With careful planning and regular contributions, you'll be well-prepared to checkmate any financial challenges in your golden years, enjoying a comfortable and secure retirement.

The Power Of Compound Interest

One of the most magical concepts in long-term investing is compound interest. It's like a snowball rolling down a hill, gathering more snow and growing bigger as it goes. When you invest, you earn interest on your initial investment. Over time, you start earning interest on your interest, and the cycle continues. The longer you invest, the more powerful this effect becomes. It's the financial equivalent of a perpetual motion machine, working tirelessly to grow your wealth.

Imagine compound interest as the magical force in the realm of finance. It's like a tiny snowball that you start rolling at the top of a hill. At first, it seems small and insignificant, but as it rolls down, it gathers more snow, growing larger and faster. This snowball effect is the essence of compound interest.

When you first invest, you earn interest on your initial amount—your principal. But here's where the magic happens: that interest doesn't just sit there. It gets added to your principal, and then you start earning interest on the new, larger amount. Over time, this cycle repeats, and your investment grows exponentially. It's like watching a snowball transform into a giant snow boulder, gaining momentum and size with each turn.

The true power of compound interest lies in its ability to turn time into a valuable ally. The longer you keep your money invested, the more pronounced the compounding effect becomes. It's like planting a seed that grows into a tree, which then produces more seeds, leading to a flourishing forest over the years. Each year your money stays invested, it has the potential to grow even more, creating a snowball effect that accelerates your wealth accumulation.

Think of compound interest as a perpetual motion machine in the financial world. Once set in motion, it works tirelessly to grow your wealth, requiring minimal effort from you. All you need is patience and time. The earlier you start investing, the more powerful the compounding effect will be. It's like giving your snowball a head start at the highest point on the hill, ensuring it gathers maximum momentum on its way down.

To truly harness the power of compound interest, consistency is key. Regular contributions to your investments act like fresh snow added to your growing snowball, accelerating its growth. Even small, regular investments can lead to significant wealth over time, thanks to the magic of compounding.

So, embrace the wonder of compound interest. Start early, invest consistently, and watch as your money transforms, rolling down the hill and growing bigger with each passing year. It's the financial equivalent of a perpetual motion machine, tirelessly working to secure your financial future and build your wealth.

Staying The Course

Investing for long-term goals requires patience and discipline. There will be ups and downs, but it's crucial to stay the course. Imagine running a marathon; there are moments when you feel invincible, and others when you're just trying to keep going. The key is to maintain a steady pace and keep your eyes on the prize. Don't let short-term market fluctuations scare you into making impulsive decisions. Remember, you're in this for the long haul.

Think of long-term investing as running a marathon, not a sprint. In a marathon, there are times when you're in the zone, feeling like you could run forever. But there are also moments when every step is a struggle, and you're just trying to push through the pain. Investing is much the same. There will be periods when your portfolio is growing steadily, and you feel on top of the world. But there will also be downturns, when the market dips and your investments take a hit.

The key to success is maintaining a steady pace and staying focused on your long-term goals. It's like keeping your eyes on the finish line, no matter how far away it seems. When the market gets turbulent, it's easy to panic and consider pulling out your investments. But remember, the best marathon runners don't quit at the first sign of fatigue. They keep moving forward, knowing that perseverance is the key to reaching the finish line.

Short-term market fluctuations are like the hills and valleys of your marathon route. They're challenging, but they're also temporary. Just as you wouldn't abandon a marathon because of a steep hill, you shouldn't abandon your long-term investment strategy because of a market dip. Staying the course means trusting that these ups and downs are part of the journey, and that over time, your investments will grow.

Patience and discipline are your greatest allies. Think of them as the mental fortitude that keeps marathon runners going. By sticking to your investment plan and avoiding impulsive decisions, you allow your money the time it needs to compound and grow. It's this steady, unwavering approach that turns short-term setbacks into long-term gains.

To help stay the course, it's useful to remind yourself why you're investing in the first place. Whether it's for a comfortable retirement, your children's education, or a dream home, keeping your goals in mind can provide the motivation you need to stay committed. It's like visualizing yourself crossing the marathon finish line, arms raised in victory.

So, embrace the marathon mindset in your investment journey. Stay patient, disciplined, and focused on your long-term goals. Don't let short-term fluctuations derail your plans. By staying the course, you'll navigate the ups and downs and ultimately achieve the financial success you're aiming for.

Automating Your Investments

Just like with short-term savings, automating your investments can be a game-changer. Set up automatic contributions to your retirement accounts or investment portfolios. This ensures you're consistently investing without having to think about it. It's like having a personal trainer who keeps you on track with your fitness goals. Plus, automating your investments takes advantage of dollar-cost averaging, which means you're buying more shares when prices are low and fewer when prices are high, potentially lowering your overall cost per share over time.

Imagine automating your investments as hiring a diligent personal trainer for your finances. This trainer makes sure you never miss a workout (or in this case, an investment), keeping you on track towards your financial fitness goals. By setting up automatic contributions to your retirement accounts or investment portfolios, you ensure that a portion of your income is consistently invested, month after month, without you having to lift a finger.

This automated approach takes the guesswork and emotional decision-making out of investing. It's like putting your investments on autopilot, allowing you to focus on other aspects of your life while your money steadily grows. Automation helps you stick to your investment plan, much like how a personal trainer keeps you committed to your fitness regimen, ensuring you don't skip those crucial workout sessions.

One of the biggest advantages of automating your investments is that it leverages the power of dollar-cost averaging. This strategy involves investing a fixed amount of money at regular intervals, regardless of the market's performance. When prices are low, your fixed contribution buys more shares; when prices are high, it buys fewer shares. Over time, this can potentially lower your average cost per share, smoothing out the effects of market volatility.

Think of dollar-cost averaging as your financial safety net, helping you avoid the pitfalls of trying to time the market. Just as a steady exercise routine builds muscle and endurance over time, consistent investing helps grow your wealth and mitigate risks. By automatically investing a set amount regularly, you benefit from the long-term growth potential of the market while reducing the impact of short-term fluctuations.

Automating your investments also brings peace of mind. You no longer need to worry about missing a contribution or finding the perfect time to invest. It's like setting up a self-sustaining system that works tirelessly in the background, ensuring your financial goals are met. This hands-off approach allows you to stay focused on your long-term objectives, confident that your investments are being taken care of.

So, embrace the power of automation in your investment strategy. Set up automatic contributions to your retirement accounts or investment portfolios and let this financial personal trainer keep you on track. With automation, you'll consistently invest, take advantage of dollar-cost averaging, and steadily work towards building a robust financial future, all with minimal effort on your part.

Diversifying Your Portfolio

Diversification is the practice of spreading your investments across different asset classes, industries, and geographies to reduce risk. It's like not putting all your eggs in one basket. If one investment performs poorly, others might do well, balancing out your overall returns. A well-diversified portfolio includes a mix of stocks, bonds, real estate, and other assets, ensuring you're protected from the inevitable ups and downs of the market.

Imagine you're planning a grand feast. You wouldn't want to serve just one dish, would you? A plate full of only mashed potatoes might be comforting, but it's not exactly exciting. Instead, you want a variety of dishes—some savory, some sweet, a mix of textures and flavors—to delight your guests and make sure everyone finds something they enjoy. That's exactly what diversification does for your investment portfolio.

Think of diversification as your financial buffet. You've got stocks sizzling on the grill, bonds simmering in the pot, real estate roasting in the oven, and maybe even a sprinkling of exotic investments to spice things up. By spreading your investments across different asset classes, industries, and geographies, you're ensuring a well-rounded meal that can withstand any culinary disaster. If the grilled stocks come out a bit overcooked, no worries —you've still got a delicious pot of bonds to serve.

The beauty of diversification lies in its ability to balance your overall returns. It's like a see-saw that keeps your portfolio stable. When one investment takes a dip, others might rise, smoothing out the ride. This way, you're not overly reliant on a single investment's performance. It's like having a safety net in a circus act, catching you when one part of your performance doesn't go as planned.

Let's dive into the main courses of your diversified financial feast:

Stocks: These are the spicy, exciting dishes that can offer high returns but can also be a bit volatile. Think of them as the bold flavors in your buffet.

Bonds: The comfort food of your portfolio. They provide stability and steady income, much like a warm, hearty stew.

Real Estate: These are the robust, filling entrees. Real estate investments offer tangible value and potential for appreciation, adding substantial weight to your portfolio.

Other Assets: These are your exotic dishes—commodities, mutual funds, REITs, and other unique investments. They add diversity and keep things interesting.

By combining these different investment types, you create a well-balanced portfolio that's prepared for any market scenario. Diversification ensures that when one dish is a bit underwhelming, the others can still shine, providing a delightful experience overall.

So, the next time you think about your investments, picture that grand feast. Make sure you're not putting all your eggs (or mashed potatoes) in one basket. Spread them out, mix things up, and enjoy the balanced, flavorful journey towards your financial goals. Diversification is your secret recipe for a resilient, successful portfolio, ensuring you're ready for whatever the market serves up.

Regularly Reviewing Your Goals

Life is full of surprises, and your financial goals might change over time. Maybe you decide to buy a bigger house, or perhaps you want to retire earlier than planned. Regularly reviewing and adjusting your investment strategy ensures that it remains aligned with your evolving goals. It's like checking your map during a road trip to make sure you're still headed in the right direction.

Imagine you're on an epic road trip across the country. You've packed your bags, planned your route, and set off on an adventure. But as with any great journey, unexpected detours and new destinations can pop up. Perhaps you hear about a charming small town with the world's best pie, or you decide you want to take the scenic coastal route instead of the highway. To make sure you still reach your ultimate destination, you need to regularly check your map and adjust your route accordingly.

The same goes for your financial journey. Your life circumstances, priorities, and goals can change, sometimes unexpectedly. Maybe you get a promotion and decide to upgrade to a bigger house. Or perhaps you've discovered a newfound passion for travel and want to retire earlier to explore the world. Whatever the case, it's essential to regularly review your financial goals and adjust your investment strategy to stay on track.

Think of this process as your financial GPS. Just as a GPS

recalculates your route when you take a wrong turn or decide on a new stop, regularly reviewing your goals helps you navigate life's twists and turns. It ensures that your investments continue to align with your evolving aspirations, keeping you on the right path.

So, grab your financial map, set your course, and be ready to make adjustments as you go. With regular check-ins and a willingness to adapt, you'll stay on the right path, moving steadily towards your ever-evolving financial goals.

Celebrate Milestones Along The Way

Long-term investing can feel like a slog, so it's important to celebrate milestones along the way. Did you hit a new high in your retirement account? Give yourself a pat on the back! Reached a significant saving goal for your child's college fund? Treat yourself to something special. Celebrating these milestones keeps you motivated and reminds you that you're making progress, even if the finish line is still far off.

Long-term goals are the marathons of the financial world. They require patience, persistence, and a clear vision of the future you want to create. By investing in stocks, mutual funds, real estate, and retirement accounts, and harnessing the power of compound interest, you can build a solid financial foundation for the future. Stay the course, automate your investments, diversify your portfolio, and regularly review your goals. And don't forget to celebrate your achievements along the way. You've got the endurance and the strategy to reach the finish line. So lace up those running shoes and start your journey to financial success today! Understanding Your Risk Tolerance: Are You a Tortoise or a Hare?

Risk tolerance is all about how much financial uncertainty you can handle without losing sleep. It's a crucial part of your investment plan because it influences what kind of investments you make and how you react to the wild ride of market ups and downs.

The Tortoise: Slow And Steady Wins The Race

Sure, let's talk about our slow and steady friend, the Tortoise. Picture this: you're at the starting line of a race, not against a bunch of other runners, but against time itself. On one side, you've got the hares of the world, sprinting off with wild enthusiasm, chasing every shiny opportunity they see. On the other side, there's you, the Tortoise, with a steady gait and a twinkle of wisdom in your eye. You know that in the world of money and investing, it's not always about who's the fastest, but who can keep going without burning out.

As a Tortoise, your mantra is "Slow and steady wins the race." You're not here for the rollercoaster ride of the stock market, the heart-stopping drops, and the sky-high peaks. Nope, you prefer the scenic route with predictable views and a comfortable pace. Your favorite places to hang out? Bonds, CDs, and high-yield savings accounts – the reliable buddies who always have your back.

As a Tortoise, you value stability and predictability. You might not make headlines with your investment choices, but you also won't be the one losing sleep over market crashes or economic downturns. You're in it for the long haul, inching forward with a calm assurance that slow and steady truly does win the race.

So, here's to you, Tortoise! While the hares might have their moments of glory, it's your unflappable demeanor and unwavering strategy that often come out on top in the end. After all, while the hares are catching their breath, you're still moving forward, one steady step at a time.

The Rabbit: Fast And Furious With Money

Now, let's zoom over to the other side of the track and meet the Hare (Rabbit). Imagine strapping on your running shoes, feeling the rush of adrenaline as you take off at lightning speed. For you, the thrill of the chase is what it's all about. You're a risk-taker, a thrill-seeker, and the word "adventure" might as well be your middle name. If the Tortoise is all about stability, you're here to embrace the excitement of the unknown. Welcome to Hare territory!

In the world of the Hare, speed and daring rule the day. You're not afraid of a little risk if it means the potential for big rewards. The idea of seeing your money grow slowly doesn't quite match your style; you want to see those returns come in fast, even if it means dealing with a few bumps along the way.

Your playground? The fast-paced arenas of stocks, real estate, and mutual funds. Stocks are like the exhilarating rollercoasters of the financial world – one moment you're up, the next you're down, but the ride is always thrilling. Real estate? It's like a high-stakes treasure hunt, where you're always on the lookout for the next big score. And mutual funds? Think of them as a buffet of investments, where you get a taste of everything with the potential for a feast of returns.

Being a Hare means you're comfortable with a bit of chaos. You thrive on the ups and downs, the peaks and valleys. You know that while there's a chance for losses, the potential for high returns makes it all worthwhile. You're the kind of investor who isn't afraid to take bold steps, make quick decisions, and enjoy the ride, no matter how wild it gets.

So here's to you, Hare! While the Tortoise is slowly but surely making its way to the finish line, you're racing ahead, embracing every twist and turn. It's a wild world out there, but for you, it's all part of the fun. You're in it for the excitement, the thrill, and the chance to come out on top with a victorious leap.

Mixed Breed: A Little Bit Of Both

Alright, let's dive into the world of the Mixed Breed investor – a delightful blend of Tortoise and Hare. Imagine you're living the best of both worlds, balancing stability with excitement. You've got one foot in the secure, predictable realm and the other in the thrilling, high-reward zone. This approach is like having a trusty sedan for your daily commute and a flashy sports car for weekend adventures.

As a Mixed Breed, you're all about balance. You appreciate the security of safe investments that provide steady returns without too much drama. These are your bonds, CDs, and high-yield savings accounts – the dependable, always-there-for-you friends. They're like the sedan in your garage: reliable, comfortable, and perfect for those family road trips. You know they won't let you down, and they'll get you where you need to go, smoothly and safely.

But you're not all work and no play. Oh no! You've also got a taste for the excitement that comes with higher-risk, higher-reward investments. Enter the world of stocks, real estate, and mutual funds. These are your sports cars, the ones you take out when you're feeling adventurous and want to feel the wind in your hair. Sure, there's a bit more risk involved, but that's part of the thrill. You're okay with a few bumps in the road if it means you might hit the jackpot.

Your investment strategy is like planning the perfect weekend. Monday to Friday, you're all about the reliable routine, knowing your steady investments are working hard for you. But come the weekend, you're ready to let loose, take some risks, and see where the adventure leads. It's this mix of security and excitement that keeps things interesting and helps you sleep well at night.

You know that a well-balanced investment portfolio is key to long-term success. By blending the safe with the adventurous, you're not putting all your eggs in one basket. Instead, you're spreading your risk while still allowing room for growth and opportunity. It's the perfect combination of prudence and passion.

So, here's to you, Mixed Breed! You've figured out how to enjoy the best of both worlds, cruising through life with a reliable foundation and a taste for adventure. Whether you're in your sturdy sedan or your zippy sports car, you're ready for whatever the road ahead may bring..

How To Figure Out Where You Fit

Alright, let's get into the fun and fabulous world of figuring out where you fit in the investment landscape. We're going to turn this into a light-hearted adventure. Imagine you're about to take a personality quiz, but instead of discovering which Hogwarts house you belong to, you're uncovering your inner investor type. Ready? Let's dive in!

Personality Quiz Time! (Just kidding, sort of)

To start, let's think about how you deal with money matters. It's all about understanding yourself better and making investments that suit your style. Grab a cup of coffee, sit back, and ponder these questions:

1. How do you handle stress, particularly financial stress?
   - Picture this: Your car breaks down, and you need to shell out some serious cash to get it   fixed. Do you:
      - **A)** Take a deep breath, maybe do some yoga, and figure out how to handle it calmly?
      - **B)** Freak out a little, then start thinking about selling stuff on eBay to cover the cost?
      - **C)** Laugh it off, saying, "It's just money, I'll figure it out"?

2. Do you have debts or financial obligations that could affect your investing?

- Think about your monthly finances. Are you:
    - **A)** Pretty much debt-free with all bills paid on time?
    - **B)** Managing some student loans or a mortgage, but generally on top of things?
    - **C)** Juggling credit card debt and feeling like you're one unexpected expense away from a meltdown?

3. How would you react if you woke up to find your investment had dropped 10% overnight?
    - Imagine checking your investment app and seeing a significant drop. Do you:
    - **A)** Stay calm, knowing it's just a temporary dip and things will bounce back?
    - **B)** Feel a bit anxious but decide to ride it out and see what happens?
    - **C)** Panic and think about pulling out all your money immediately?

4. How long do you want to invest your money?
    - Consider your investment horizon. Are you:
    - **A)** In it for the long haul, planning to keep your money invested for many years?
    - **B)** Looking at a medium-term plan, maybe five to ten years?
    - **C)** Wanting quick returns, hoping to see results within a couple of years?

Decoding Your Answers
Now that you've thought about these questions, let's break it down.

Mostly A's: You're a Tortoise!
You're calm under pressure, financially stable, and patient. Slow and steady wins the race for you. You're probably most comfortable with low-risk investments that provide steady returns over time. Think bonds, CDs, and high-yield savings accounts. You prefer a reliable sedan that'll get you there safely, even if it's not the fastest ride.

Mostly B's: You're a Mixed Breed!
You're balanced, dealing with financial stress reasonably well and open to both secure and higher-risk investments. You have some financial obligations but manage them effectively. You're comfortable with a mix of investment types – a bit of stability combined with some high-growth opportunities. You're like someone who drives a dependable sedan during the week but loves to take the sports car out on weekends.

Mostly C's: You're a Hare!
You're adventurous, not easily rattled by financial ups and downs, and willing to take risks for the chance of higher returns. While you might have some financial obligations, you're ready to jump into the thrill of high-stakes investing. Stocks, real estate, and mutual funds are your playgrounds. You love the rush of speed and the potential for big wins, even if it means facing some bumps along the way.

Balancing Your Portfolio

Balancing Your Portfolio: Finding the Sweet Spot

Alright, now that we know whether you're a Tortoise, Hare, or Mixed Breed, let's dive into the art of balancing your portfolio. It's all about finding that sweet spot where you're comfortable and your money can grow steadily or race ahead, depending on your style. Imagine your portfolio as a buffet table where you need to have a bit of everything to make it satisfying and nutritious. Here's how you can balance it to suit your taste:

For Tortoises: Slow And Steady Savers

As a Tortoise, you love the comfort of knowing your investments are safe and sound. Here's how to keep your portfolio steady yet a little adventurous:

1. Stick to Low-Risk Investments:

- Your primary focus should be on low-risk, stable investments like bonds, CDs, and high-yield savings accounts. These are like your dependable friends who always show up on time and never let you down. They might not make you rich overnight, but they ensure your money grows steadily.

2. Diversify for Growth:

- While you prefer the safe side, adding a sprinkle of moderate-risk investments can give your portfolio a growth boost. Think about including some dividend-paying stocks or balanced mutual funds. It's like adding a bit of spice to your favorite dish – not too much, just enough to enhance the flavor.

3. Stay Informed and Adjust:

- Even if you're a Tortoise, it's important to stay updated on market trends and adjust your portfolio occasionally. This doesn't mean taking big risks, but being aware and making minor tweaks can help you stay on track without venturing too far from your comfort zone.

For Mixed Breeds: The Best Of Both Worlds

As a Mixed Breed, you enjoy a bit of excitement but also value stability. Here's how to balance your portfolio to keep things interesting and secure:

1. Foundation of Stability:

- Start with a solid foundation of low-risk investments. Bonds and CDs should form the base of your portfolio, giving you that security blanket you crave. These investments are like the dependable parts of your wardrobe – the classic jeans and comfy sweaters.

2. Sprinkle in Some Excitement:

- Add a healthy dose of higher-risk investments like stocks

and mutual funds. This is where you get to have some fun and potentially see higher returns. It's like having a little black dress or a snazzy tie – they add flair and make things interesting.

3. Adjust According to Goals:
   - Your investment strategy should reflect your financial goals and risk tolerance. If you're saving for a long-term goal like retirement, you might lean more towards stability. If you have a shorter-term goal, like buying a house in five years, you might take a few more risks. It's all about finding the right balance for your unique situation.

4. Keep an Eye on the Market:
   - Regularly review your portfolio and make adjustments as needed. This doesn't mean changing things up every week, but a yearly review can help you stay aligned with your goals. Think of it as a yearly wardrobe refresh – getting rid of what doesn't fit and adding new pieces that do.

For Hares: Thrill-Seekers With Money

Hares love the rush of high-stakes investing. If this sounds like you, here's how to keep the excitement alive while staying grounded:

1. Embrace High-Risk, High-Reward:
   - Your portfolio should have a good chunk of high-risk investments like stocks, real estate, and even some speculative investments. These are your rollercoaster rides – thrilling, potentially lucrative, but with ups and downs.

2. Don't Forget the Safety Net:
   - Even though you love the excitement, having a portion of your portfolio in low-risk investments is crucial. Think of these as your seatbelt on the rollercoaster – they keep you secure during those wild turns. Bonds and high-yield savings accounts can provide this stability.

3. Diversify to Spread Risk:

- Diversification is key to managing the risk in your portfolio. Spread your investments across different sectors and asset classes to cushion against potential losses. It's like having different rides at an amusement park – if one's closed, you still have others to enjoy.

4. Stay Informed and Agile:

- As a Hare, staying informed about market trends and being ready to make quick decisions is essential. Regularly review your portfolio and be prepared to make adjustments. It's like being a race car driver – you need to know when to accelerate and when to brake.

Final Thoughts: Finding Your Perfect Fit

Understanding your risk tolerance and investment style is crucial to creating a balanced portfolio that suits you. Whether you're a Tortoise, Hare, or Mixed Breed, the goal is to align your investments with your financial goals and comfort level. It's all about finding the perfect fit, just like a pair of shoes that's both stylish and comfortable for the journey ahead.

Steps to a Balanced Portfolio

1. Assess Your Risk Tolerance:

- Reflect on the questions we discussed earlier. How do you handle financial stress? What's your investment time frame? These insights will guide your investment strategy.

2. Set Clear Financial Goals:

- Define what you want to achieve with your investments. Are you saving for retirement, a down payment on a house, or a dream vacation? Clear goals help in crafting a strategy that's tailored to your needs.

3. Diversify Your Investments:

- Don't put all your eggs in one basket. Spread your investments across different asset classes and sectors. This helps minimize risk while maximizing potential returns.

4. Regularly Review and Adjust:
- Make it a habit to review your portfolio at least once a year. Adjust your investments based on market changes and your evolving financial goals. This keeps your portfolio aligned and dynamic.

5. Stay Informed:
- Keep learning about the financial markets and investment strategies. The more informed you are, the better decisions you'll make. Read, watch, listen – knowledge is power.

6. Seek Professional Advice if Needed:
- If you're unsure about making investment decisions, don't hesitate to seek advice from financial advisors. They can provide personalized guidance based on your unique situation.

Setting Smart Investment Goals

Let's talk about setting goals – SMART goals, to be precise. These aren't just any goals; they're Specific, Measurable, Achievable, Relevant, and Time-bound. SMART goals are like a roadmap for your financial journey, guiding you step-by-step to your destination. Let's dive in and see how you can set SMART goals for your investments in a fun and easy-to-understand way.

What Are Smart Goals?

SMART goals are a structured way to turn your financial dreams into actionable steps:

- Specific: Define exactly what you want to achieve.
- Measurable: Determine how you'll track your progress.
- Achievable: Set realistic and attainable goals.

- Relevant: Ensure your goals align with your priorities.
- Time-bound: Set a deadline to create a sense of urgency.

Now, let's see how you can apply these principles to your investment goals.
Example: Buying a Home
Imagine you have a dream of buying a cozy home. Here's how to set a SMART goal for this dream:

1. Specific: "I want to buy a home."
2. Measurable: "I need $40,000 for a down payment."
3. Achievable: "I will invest $500 a month."
4. Relevant: "Buying a home is a priority for my family's stability."
5. Time-bound: "I aim to reach this goal in five years."

When you put it all together, your SMART goal looks like this: "I want to buy a home and need $40,000 for a down payment. I will invest $500 a month to achieve this goal within five years because buying a home is a priority for my family's stability."

Applying SMART Goals to Other Dreams

The beauty of SMART goals is their versatility. Here are a few more examples:

1. Saving for Retirement:
    - Specific: "I want to retire comfortably."
    - Measurable: "I need $1 million in my retirement fund."
    - Achievable: "I will invest $800 a month."
    - Relevant: "Retirement savings is crucial for my future security."
    - Time-bound: "I aim to achieve this goal in 25 years."

2. Planning a Dream Vacation:
    - Specific: "I want to go on a two-week vacation to Europe."
    - Measurable: "I need $10,000."
    - Achievable: "I will save $200 a month."
    - Relevant: "Taking this trip is important for my personal fulfillment."

- Time-bound: "I aim to save this amount within four years."

Tips For Staying On Track

1. Regular Check-ins:
 - Schedule regular reviews to track your progress. Monthly or quarterly check-ins can help you stay focused and motivated.

2. Adjust When Needed:
 - Life happens, so be flexible. Adjust your goals if your financial situation changes or new opportunities arise.

3. Stay Motivated:
 - Keep your goals visible. Write them down and place them where you'll see them daily. Remind yourself why these goals matter to you.

Setting SMART investment goals is like creating a detailed map for your financial journey. It transforms vague dreams into clear, actionable steps that guide you toward success. Whether you're saving for a home, planning a dream vacation, or preparing for retirement, SMART goals provide the structure and motivation you need to achieve your dreams.

So, grab that pen and paper (or your favorite note-taking app), and start setting your SMART goals today. With a clear plan in place, you'll be well on your way to turning your financial dreams into reality. Happy investing! The Adventure Begins

Setting your investment goals is like setting the GPS before a road trip. It doesn't just guide you; it helps you make adjustments along the way and ensures you reach your destination. Now that you have your map and know your vehicle (your risk tolerance), you're ready to hit the road. In the next chapters, we'll dive into how to start investing

Ready, Set, Invest!

Now that you've got the basics, it's time to take the plunge. Whether you're setting up a low-risk nest egg, mixing things up with a balanced portfolio, or racing ahead with high-risk investments, the key is to stay true to your style and goals.

So, grab that trusty sedan, hop into your sports car, or do a bit of both. The road to financial success is a journey, and with the right strategy, you'll enjoy the ride. Happy investing!

CHAPTER 3: STARTING YOUR INVESTMENT JOURNEY ON A SHOESTRING BUDGET

Welcome to the Bootstrap Investor Club

Congratulations! You've made it to the chapter where your piggy bank goes from empty to entrepreneurial! Now, let's face it, not all of us have a mountain of cash lying around, waiting to be invested. Most of us are dealing with more of a small hill... or a flat surface. But fear not! Today, we're going to turn those tiny piles of cash into your future empire, one dollar at a time.

So, welcome to the Bootstrap Investor Club, where scrappy, savvy, and smart are our middle names. You might not have a vault full of gold coins like Scrooge McDuck, but who needs that when you've got determination, creativity, and a touch of financial wizardry? It's time to roll up those sleeves and get to work, because here in the Bootstrap Club, every penny counts, and every penny can grow.

Picture this: Your piggy bank is more like a hungry little piglet, squealing for those spare coins from your pocket. Feed it well, and it will grow into a mighty hog that can take on the world! We're talking about the ultimate glow-up for your finances. It's time to give those coins a job – not just any job, but a job with benefits, a 401(k), and room for growth.

First, let's tackle the myth that you need a ton of money to start investing. Nope, not true! Even if you're dealing with what feels like pocket change, those nickels and dimes can add up. Think of them as the tiny seeds that, with the right care and attention, will grow into a lush money tree. And who doesn't want a money tree?

As a member of the Bootstrap Investor Club, you're not just another investor. You're a financial alchemist, turning base coins into golden opportunities. It's all about starting small, thinking big, and being consistent. Remember, every great empire started with a single step – or in this case, a single dollar.

So, embrace your inner Bootstrapper, feed that piggy bank, and let's get investing. Your future empire awaits, and it's going to be legendary! H

Budgeting For Investment: Squeezing Your Dollars Until They Holler

Before we can start multiplying your money, we need to find some money to multiply. That's where budgeting comes in. Think of budgeting not as a financial diet but more like a map to hidden treasure. Here's how to start digging:

1. Track Your Treasure (and Trash)
For one month, keep track of every coin you spend. Yes, even that emergency chocolate bar purchase. This isn't just about figuring out where your money is going; it's about finding out where it could be going instead. Consider yourself a financial detective,

on the lookout for those sneaky little expenses that add up. Did you really need that second latte? Probably not. But hey, we're all human.

2. Categorize Your Cash

Sure, here's a fun and engaging way to explain categorizing your cash:

Alright, it's time to put on your sharpest suit and step into the role of the CFO of your life. Imagine you're in the boardroom, ready to conduct a budget audit. The first step? Categorizing your cash. Breaking down your expenses into clear categories can be an eye-opener—like realizing you've been feeding a small country with your snack budget.

Needs: The Essentials

First up, we have the essentials, or what we call "Needs." These are the must-haves that keep your life running smoothly: rent, utilities, groceries, and any other non-negotiable expenses. Think of them as the backbone of your budget, ensuring you have a roof over your head, food on the table, and the lights on.

Wants: The Fun Stuff

Next, we have "Wants," the fun stuff that adds sparkle to your life. This includes dining out, entertainment, hobbies, and those impulse buys that make you smile. These are like the cherry on top of your financial sundae—nice to have but not essential. It's crucial to keep an eye on this category because it's where money can disappear faster than a magician's assistant.

Savings/Investments: Future Best Friend

Finally, we have "Savings/Investments," the category dedicated to Future You. This is where you allocate funds for your savings goals, investments, and emergency fund. Think of it as sending love letters to your future self, ensuring you're prepared for whatever life throws your way and building a nest egg for long-term dreams.

The Big Picture

When you lay out your expenses in these categories, it's like creating a financial blueprint. You might be surprised to see where your money is going—perhaps you're spending more on coffee runs than you realized, or maybe those spontaneous shopping sprees are adding up. This clarity can help you make informed decisions, trim the fat, and redirect funds toward what truly matters.

So, channel your inner CFO, grab your calculator, and start categorizing your cash. With a clear picture of your spending, you can make smarter choices, save more, and ensure your financial future is on solid ground. Plus, who knows? You might even discover that cutting back on snacks can fund that dream vacation you've been eyeing!

3. Trim the Fat

Look for places where you can cut back without shedding tears. Maybe swap a few restaurant meals for home-cooked masterpieces? Or perhaps cancel that gym membership in favor of nature walks and free YouTube fitness gurus? Think of it as a spring cleaning for your wallet. You're not giving up the things you love; you're just being smarter about how you spend. For instance, you might discover that your daily Starbucks habit costs as much as a weekend getaway over the course of a year. Yikes!

4. Automate Your Ambitions

Set up automatic transfers to your savings or investment account right after payday. It's like playing a financial game of "out of sight, out of mind"—but in a good way. You can't miss what you never saw lounging in your checking account. Automating your savings is the secret sauce to building wealth without even thinking about it. It's like having a personal assistant who stashes away your cash before you get the chance to spend it on yet another pair of shoes.

The Magic of Micro-Investing

Alright, so you've squeezed your dollars until they holler. Now, let's put those hard-earned savings to work. Enter micro-investing – the modern marvel that lets you start investing with pocket change. Picture this: every time you buy something, the app rounds up the amount to the nearest dollar and invests the difference. Bought a coffee for $2.75? Boom, 25 cents goes into your investment account. It's like a financial ninja move, silently and effectively growing your wealth.

Embrace the Spare Change Strategy

Don't underestimate the power of spare change. Those dimes and quarters can add up to significant amounts over time. Apps like Acorns or Stash are designed to help you invest small amounts regularly. They take the "I don't have enough money to invest" excuse and toss it right out the window. You'll be surprised at how quickly those small contributions grow.

Side Hustles: Your Ticket to Extra Cash

If you're serious about boosting your investment game, consider picking up a side hustle. Whether it's freelancing, selling handmade crafts, or driving for a rideshare company, there are plenty of ways to earn extra cash. This additional income can be funneled directly into your investment account, accelerating your journey toward financial freedom.

Find Your Niche

What are you good at? Maybe you're a whiz with graphic design, or perhaps you've got a knack for baking delicious cookies. Turn your talents into a money-making side gig. Platforms like Fiverr, Etsy, and Upwork offer opportunities to sell your skills and products to a global audience. Not only will you earn extra cash, but you'll also gain valuable experience and possibly discover a new passion.

Budgeting Tools: Your New Best Friends

There are numerous budgeting tools and apps available to help you manage your finances with ease. Apps like Mint, YNAB (You Need a Budget), and PocketGuard can simplify the budgeting process, track your spending, and even alert you when you're overspending in a particular category. It's like having a financial advisor in your pocket, guiding you every step of the way.

Celebrate Small Wins
Every time you reach a savings milestone, no matter how small, take a moment to celebrate. Did you save $100 this month? Fantastic! Treat yourself to a small reward, like a nice dinner or a movie night. Celebrating these small victories keeps you motivated and reminds you that you're making progress, one step at a time.

Budgeting for investment might sound like a daunting task, but with the right mindset, it can be an empowering and even fun process. Remember, it's not about depriving yourself but about making smart choices that align with your financial goals. By tracking your spending, categorizing your expenses, trimming the fat, and automating your savings, you'll find that you have more money to invest than you thought possible.

As a Bootstrap Investor, you're on a mission to turn small savings into significant wealth. Embrace the journey, celebrate your progress, and keep your eyes on the prize. Your financial future is bright, and with each dollar you wisely manage, you're one step closer to achieving your dreams. So, let's squeeze those dollars until they holler and make your money work for you.

The Power Of Consistency

One of the most crucial elements of successful investing is consistency. It's not about making huge contributions occasionally but about making regular, smaller contributions over time. Think of it as planting a garden. You don't just water your plants once and expect them to flourish. You need to tend to them regularly, giving them the care they need to grow strong and healthy. The same goes for your investments. Regular, consistent contributions, no matter how small, can grow into a significant sum over time. It's the magic of compounding at work, turning your small, steady inputs into a robust financial future.

Investment Platforms Suitable for Small Amounts: Your Low-Cost Launchpad

The New Age Of Investing

Gone are the days when investing was just for the monocle-wearing millionaires in top hats. Thanks to technology, investing is now accessible to everyone, even those starting with just a few dollars. This chapter will introduce you to some of your best friends in the investing world, from online brokers to robo-advisors and micro-investing apps.

Investing used to be an exclusive club, where only the wealthy and well-connected could join the party. Picture smoky rooms, whispered secrets, and a lot of money changing hands. Today, it's a democratized landscape where anyone with a smartphone and a few dollars can start investing. This evolution has empowered a new generation of investors to take control of their financial futures, breaking down barriers and making the stock market accessible to all.

Online Brokers: The Diy Route

Online brokers are like the self-checkout lines of investing. They give you the tools to pick and choose your investments without the need for human interaction. Perfect for the do-it-yourselfer, these platforms offer a range of features that make investing straightforward and convenient.

Robinhood: The Cool, Tech-Savvy Friend
Robinhood is famous for its zero-commission trades and user-friendly interface. It's like that cool, tech-savvy friend who gets

you into the hottest clubs for free. You can start investing with no account minimums and a sleek mobile app that makes the process almost fun. Robinhood's appeal lies in its simplicity and accessibility, making it ideal for beginners who want to dive into the world of investing without any barriers.

- **Pros:** No commissions, easy-to-use interface, access to stocks, ETFs, options, and cryptocurrencies.
- **Cons:** Limited research tools, no retirement accounts.

Webull: A Bit More Sophisticated
Webull is similar to Robinhood but with a few more bells and whistles. It offers a slightly more sophisticated platform for those who might want to get a bit more involved in their investments. With features like extended trading hours and in-depth market data, Webull is like having a friend who knows all the insider tips and tricks. It's perfect for those who want a bit more than just the basics and are ready to explore more advanced investing tools.

- **Pros:** No commissions, advanced charting tools, extended trading hours.
- **Cons:** More complex interface, no mutual funds or bonds.

Robo-Advisors: The Set-It-and-Forget-It Approach
Robo-advisors are like having a financial butler; they do most of the work for you, from picking your investments to rebalancing your portfolio. All you need to do is feed them a bit of cash now and then, and they handle the rest.

Betterment: Your Friendly Neighborhood Robot
Betterment has no minimum investment and low fees, making it as beginner-friendly as it gets. It's like your friendly neighborhood robot who's always there to help. Betterment takes your financial goals and risk tolerance into account and builds a diversified portfolio for you. It automatically rebalances your portfolio and reinvests dividends, ensuring your investments are always optimized.

- **Pros:** No minimum investment, low fees, automatic rebalancing.
- **Cons:** Limited control over specific investments.

Wealthfront: The Financial Planning Assistant
Wealthfront also has low fees and no minimum investment, but it goes a step further by offering financial planning advice along with your investments. It's like having a financial planning assistant who helps you map out your financial journey while managing your investments. Wealthfront provides tools to help you plan for major life events like buying a house or saving for college, all while managing your investment portfolio.

- **Pros:** Low fees, financial planning tools, tax-loss harvesting.
- **Cons:** Limited control over specific investments, fees for accounts over $10,000.

Acorns: The Magical Piggy Bank
Acorns is probably the best-known app in this category. It rounds up your change and puts it into a portfolio of ETFs. It's like a magical piggy bank that grows without you having to think about it. Simply link your credit or debit card, and watch your investments grow with every purchase you make. Acorns also offers features like Acorns Later, which helps you invest for retirement, and Acorns Spend, a checking account with investment integration.

- **Pros:** Automatic round-ups, easy to use, diversified portfolios.
- **Cons:** Monthly fees can be high for small balances, limited investment options.

Stash: Control Freak's Dream
Stash is similar to Acorns but with a bit more control over where your money goes. Stash lets you choose from a variety of ETFs and individual stocks, making it perfect for those who want to have a say in their investments. It's like having a customizable piggy bank that lets you decide where to invest your spare change. Stash also offers educational content to help you make informed

investment decisions.

- **Pros:** More control over investments, educational resources, low starting minimum.
- **Cons:** Monthly fees, limited investment options compared to traditional brokers.

Empowering Yourself Through Small Investments
Starting small doesn't mean thinking small. Each dollar you invest is like planting a seed. At first, it might not look like much, but given time and care, it can grow into something substantial. The key is to keep feeding your investment garden with whatever you can spare, even if it's just a few dollars at a time. Remember, it's the consistency and the habit of investing that counts the most.

.Celebrate Your Wins
Again and again, as you embark on your investment journey, remember to celebrate your milestones, no matter how small. Did you save your first $100? Fantastic! Reached your first investment goal? Amazing! These small victories keep you motivated and remind you that you're making progress. Celebrate with a small treat, like a nice dinner or a night out. It's important to acknowledge your achievements and enjoy the journey.

Keep Learning And Growing

The world of investing is constantly evolving, and there's always something new to learn. Stay curious and keep educating yourself about different investment strategies, market trends, and financial management tips. The more you know, the better equipped you'll be to make informed decisions and grow your wealth. Whether you're reading books, attending workshops, or following financial blogs, continuous learning is key to your success as an investor.

Your Financial Future Awaits

You've got the tools, the knowledge, and the motivation to succeed. Now it's time to take action and start building your financial future. Remember, every great journey begins with a single step. As a Bootstrap Investor, you're well on your way to turning those small savings into significant wealth. Embrace the process, stay consistent, and keep your eyes on the prize. Your financial empire is just a few smart decisions away.

CHAPTER 4: THE MECHANICS OF INVESTING: FROM OPENING ACCOUNTS TO OUTSMARTING TAXES

Welcome to the Workshop of Wealth!

If investing is an art, then opening an investment account is like setting up your easel, and understanding fees and taxes is like making sure you don't accidentally paint over a masterpiece with coffee instead of varnish. Let's dive into the nuts and bolts, the gears and cogs of the investing machinery!

Step 1: Opening An Investment Account – Like Setting Up A Social Media Profile, But For Money

Imagine opening an investment account as if you're creating a profile on "Moneybook" or "Instacash." It's your grand entrance into the financial world, and it's easier than you might think!

Step-By-Step Guide:

Step 1: Choose Your Platform
This is like picking the perfect dance floor where you'll showcase your best moves. Do you prefer a robo-advisor (think: the automated DJ), an online broker (the classic dance hall), or a micro-investing app (the trendy club)? Each platform has its own rhythm, so choose the one that gets your toes tapping.

Step 2: Gather Your Gear
Before you can start grooving, you need to gather some essentials: your ID (to prove you're you), your Social Security number (it's like your unique dance move), and your bank details (so you can transfer money into your investment account without resorting to carrier pigeons).

Step 3: Fill Out the Forms
This step is just like signing up for your favorite online service. You'll enter your details honestly—this isn't about impressing anyone with a glamorous profile pic, it's about getting your financial information right.

Step 4: Decide on Your Investment Type
Now, it's time to choose your financial toppings. Will it be stocks, bonds, or a delightful mix? Think of it like picking your favorite frozen yogurt flavors and toppings. Don't worry, you can always switch things up later if you crave something new (and there's no risk of sticky fingers here).

Step 5: Fund Your Account
This part is like feeding coins into a magic bean machine. Transfer some money into your account and watch it start to grow. These beans might not sprout overnight, but with patience, they can grow into something substantial. Just like keeping up with your

social media posts, regularly adding money to your investment account can help it grow steadily. Think of it as nurturing your financial garden with regular watering.

Step 6: Start Investing!
Congratulations! You're now ready to buy your first shares. It's like planting a small acorn and watching it grow into a mighty oak. Your money is on its way to becoming something big and strong.

So, there you have it! Opening an investment account is straightforward and can be as fun as setting up your next social media profile. Get ready to make your money moves and watch your financial future take off! Happy investing! Step 2: Understanding Fees – Because Even Superheroes Need to Get Paid

Understanding Investment Fees: The Cost Of Being A Financial Superhero

Investing isn't free, much like superheroes need to buy capes and gadgets. Understanding fees is crucial because they can eat into your profits like a sneaky cookie monster. Let's break down the types of fees in a fun and simple way:

Types Of Fees:

1. Transaction Fees
Every time you buy or sell a stock, you might pay a transaction fee. It's like a toll on a highway; it's annoying, but it gets you where you need to go. Imagine you're a superhero flying across the city—each time you swoop down to save the day, there's a small fee for using the city's airspace.

2. Management Fees
If you're using a robo-advisor or a mutual fund, there's a fee for managing your investments. It's like paying a wizard to keep your treasure safe and growing. Think of it as hiring a magical guardian

who ensures your gold coins multiply while you focus on other heroic deeds.

3. Annual Fees
Some accounts charge an annual fee, like a club membership, keeping your account active and serviced. It's similar to paying yearly dues to stay in the Justice League. These fees ensure your investment platform remains top-notch and ready to support your financial missions.

4. Performance Fees
Some fancy investment funds charge a performance fee if they do really well. It's like tipping your chef if your dinner was out-of-this-world delicious. Imagine your investments as a high-stakes poker game; if your manager wins big for you, they take a small cut as a reward for their expert skills.

5. Load Fees
These are charged by some mutual funds when you buy or sell your shares. Front-load fees are taken when you buy, and back-load fees when you sell. It's like a cover charge at a club, either on your way in or your way out. Picture yourself as a superhero attending a fancy gala—sometimes there's an entry fee, and sometimes you pay when you leave after a night of saving the world.

Why Fees Matter:

Understanding these fees is crucial because they can impact your overall returns. Here's a fun analogy: imagine you're baking a cake (your investment). Each fee is like an ingredient you have to pay for. Too many expensive ingredients, and your cake (profit) might not turn out as big as you hoped. But by being aware of the costs, you can budget wisely and still whip up something delicious.

Tips To Manage Fees:

Do Your Research:
- Before choosing an investment platform or fund, compare fees. Look for options with lower costs, especially if you're just starting out. It's like comparing superhero gadgets; you want the best value for your money.

Consider No-Load Funds:
- No-load mutual funds don't charge load fees. Choosing these funds can help you avoid unnecessary costs. Think of it as finding a secret passage to your superhero hideout—no entry fee required!

Use Discount Brokers:
- Many online brokers offer lower transaction fees compared to traditional brokers. These platforms can help you save money, much like finding a budget-friendly gadget supplier.

Watch for Hidden Fees:
- Read the fine print to uncover any hidden fees that might surprise you later. It's like being on the lookout for traps set by villains; stay vigilant to protect your profits.

Automate to Save:
- Some platforms offer lower fees if you set up automatic investments. It's like having a sidekick who helps you invest regularly, ensuring you stay on track without incurring extra costs.

By understanding and managing these fees, you can keep more of your hard-earned money working for you. Just like a savvy superhero who knows the ins and outs of their gear, you'll be better equipped to navigate the investment world and build your financial empire. Happy investing! Step 3: Navigating the Tax Jungle – It's Less Scary With a Good Guide

Investing can feel like a walk in a beautiful park until you meet the tax bear. Here's how to deal with this growly beast without losing your picnic basket.

Basic Tax Implications: Making Taxes Fun (Sort Of)

Taxes might not be the most exciting topic, but understanding them can save you money. Let's break down the basics with some humor to keep it light and easy to understand.

Capital Gains Tax

When you sell your investments for more than you bought them for, you'll pay capital gains tax on the profit. It's like baking a delicious victory cake and having to give a slice to the government. You get to enjoy the cake, but Uncle Sam gets his piece too.

Short-term gains: If you sell an investment you've held for a year or less, you'll pay a higher tax rate, like ordinary income tax. It's like eating your cake too soon and having to pay a higher price for the rush.
Long-term gains: Hold your investment for more than a year, and you'll pay a lower tax rate. It's like letting your cake cool properly and enjoying it at a leisurely pace.

Dividend Tax

Some stocks pay dividends, which is like the company sharing its profits with you. This extra cash is also taxable. Imagine finding money on the street and then having to report it to the authorities. It's free money, but with a catch.

Qualified dividends: These are taxed at the lower long-term capital gains rates. It's like getting a discounted tax rate because you're a loyal customer.
Ordinary dividends: These are taxed at your regular income tax rate. It's like paying full price because you're just another customer.

Interest Tax

If you earn interest from bonds or savings accounts, that's taxable too. Yes, even your money's money gets taxed. Think of it as your cash earning a little extra, only to find out that the taxman wants a share of that extra as well. It's like finding out your pet hamster has to pay rent for its little wheel.

Tax-Advantaged Accounts

Some accounts, like Roth IRAs or 401(k)s, offer tax benefits. These accounts either let you invest pre-tax money or let your investments grow tax-free. It's like having a secret path through the tax woods, where the taxman can't follow. You get to keep more of your money, which is always a win.

Traditional Ira/401(K):

You contribute pre-tax money, which means you get a tax break now, but you'll pay taxes when you withdraw the money in retirement. It's like deferring your tax snack for a full meal later.
Roth IRA/401(k):You contribute post-tax money, which means you pay taxes now, but your money grows tax-free, and withdrawals in retirement are tax-free too. It's like paying for your snack upfront but then enjoying endless refills without any extra charge.

By understanding these basic tax implications, you can make smarter investment decisions and keep more of your hard-earned money. Taxes might not be thrilling, but with the right knowledge, you can handle them like a pro. Happy investing and tax-saving!
 And as always, when in doubt, consult a tax professional. They're like your financial sidekick, helping you navigate the tricky parts.

Wrapping It Up: Keeping It Simple, Fun, And Profitable

Remember, the goal here is to make investing as simple and fun as possible. Think of yourself as a financial explorer. You've just set up camp, learned how to read your map, and understood how to keep your provisions safe from wild animals (or wild taxes). With your account set up and a solid understanding of the fees and taxes involved, you're ready to embark on your investment adventure.

You've tackled the basics: setting up your investment account, understanding the various types of fees, and navigating the tax implications of your investments. Each step you've taken is a milestone on your journey towards financial empowerment. Just like a savvy explorer, you've equipped yourself with the tools and knowledge needed to traverse the investment landscape with confidence.

Remember to keep track of your transactions, stay informed about changes in tax laws, and don't hesitate to seek advice from a financial professional when needed. These strategies will help you maximize your returns and minimize surprises along the way.

Investing doesn't have to be daunting. By breaking it down into manageable steps and adding a touch of consistency, you can make the process enjoyable and rewarding. So, keep your eyes on the horizon, celebrate your small victories, and stay committed to your goals. Your financial future is bright, and you're well on your way to making your money work for you.

Happy investing, and may your financial journey be as exciting and profitable as you've imagined!

CHAPTER 5: THE ART OF DIVERSIFICATION: OR HOW TO NOT PUT ALL YOUR EGGS IN ONE BASKET

Welcome to the Mixing Bowl of Money

Imagine you're at a grand buffet, one where every dish is as tempting as the next. Would you pile your plate with just spaghetti, ignoring the steak, salad, and perhaps, the chocolate fountain? Probably not. Diversifying your investments is a lot like balancing your plate at a buffet. It's about not committing all your resources to one option, no matter how much you love spaghetti.

Now, picture this: You're strolling down the buffet line, and your eyes widen at the array of choices. There's crispy fried chicken, a vibrant vegetable medley, creamy mashed potatoes, and a rainbow of desserts. If you stick to just one dish, you miss out on the full experience. Plus, who wants to be the person who only eats mashed potatoes at a buffet? Mixing it up not only makes your meal more exciting, but it also means you won't be devastated if one dish turns out to be a bit bland.

Investing works the same way. By spreading your money across different investments, you're not putting all your eggs in one basket. Sure, that basket might be filled with golden eggs (we're looking at you, tech stocks), but what happens if it suddenly tips over? By adding some bonds, real estate, and maybe a sprinkle of international stocks to your portfolio, you're setting yourself up for a more balanced and potentially more rewarding financial future.

Think of it as creating a financial feast. Each type of investment adds a different flavor to your overall portfolio. Some are spicy, some are sweet, and some are comforting and steady. The key is to enjoy a little bit of everything, ensuring that if one dish doesn't quite hit the mark, you've got plenty of other tasty options to keep you satisfied. So, let's dive into the how and why of mixing it up!

The Magic Of Diversification: Your Financial Safety Net

Why Diversify?

Think of investing like a talent show. If you put all your money into one stock (or one performer), and they forget their lines or trip over their feet, your investment night is ruined. But, if you spread your bets across various acts—from jugglers (bonds) to singers (stocks) and magicians (real estate)—one flubbed performance won't spell disaster for your entire evening.

Now, imagine you're the judge of this talent show. Each performer has their unique flair: the acrobats (startups) bring excitement, the classical musicians (blue-chip stocks) offer stability, and the comedians (real estate) provide steady laughs. If you place all your hopes on just one act and they don't deliver, you're left disappointed. But, with a diverse lineup, you ensure that the show goes on, with plenty of highlights to keep the audience cheering.

Diversification is your strategy to reduce risk. It's like having different players on your team in a game of financial dodgeball. If one gets knocked out (a company tanks or a sector slumps), you've got other players ready to keep you in the game. Imagine you've got a mix of players: some fast and agile (tech stocks), some strong and dependable (bonds), and some with surprising tricks up their sleeves (real estate). Each one brings something unique to the table, ensuring you've got a well-rounded team ready to face whatever comes your way.

Think of it as creating a financial safety net. By investing in a variety of assets, you're weaving together different threads to create a strong, resilient net. If one thread breaks, the others hold strong, keeping you secure. This way, even if one part of your investment portfolio falters, the rest can support and stabilize your overall financial position. So, whether it's a talent show, a dodgeball game, or a safety net, diversification is your key to a balanced, less risky investment journey.

Crafting Your Diversified Portfolio: A Balancing Act

Creating a well-rounded investment portfolio isn't just for the wealthy or the Wall Street wizards. Even with a modest sum, you can build a portfolio that covers various asset classes, sectors, and geographies. Here's how to balance your investment plate:

Step 1: Assess Your Ingredients
Before you dive into the world of investing, the first and most crucial step is to assess your ingredients. Think of it as taking stock of your kitchen pantry before whipping up a gourmet meal. You need to know what you have, what you need, and what you can realistically achieve with the ingredients at your disposal.

Start with what you have. This means taking a thorough look at your current financial situation. How much money do you have saved up? What are your monthly income and expenses? Do you have any debts or existing investments? Understanding your financial baseline is essential because it sets the foundation for your investment journey. Just like a chef wouldn't start cooking without knowing what's in the pantry, you shouldn't start investing without knowing your financial starting point.

Next, consider what you need. What are your financial goals? Are you saving for retirement, a down payment on a house, or perhaps your child's education? Each goal might require a different approach and timeline. Knowing your goals helps you determine the types of investments that are best suited to achieve them. It's like deciding whether you're cooking a quick weeknight dinner or a lavish holiday feast—each requires different ingredients and preparation methods.

Lastly, assess your risk tolerance. How comfortable are you with taking financial risks? Are you someone who can handle market fluctuations without losing sleep, or do you prefer a more stable, predictable path? Your risk tolerance will guide your investment choices and help you balance your portfolio accordingly. Think of it as deciding how much spice you want in your dish. Some people love a little kick, while others prefer it mild. Knowing your preference will help you create a portfolio that you're comfortable with.

This assessment phase is critical because it informs every subsequent step in your investment process. By understanding your current situation, goals, and risk tolerance, you can make more informed decisions about how to allocate your resources. It's like setting a solid foundation before building a house. Without a clear assessment, you risk making investments that don't align with your needs or financial reality.

So, take your time with this step. Gather all the necessary

information and reflect on what you truly want to achieve. A well-thought-out assessment will pave the way for a successful and fulfilling investment journey.

Step 2: Choose Your Mix

Here's a simple way to think about it:

Imagine your investment portfolio as a dynamic circus performance, with each type of investment playing a unique and vital role in the show. Balancing these elements can create a spectacular, well-rounded performance that is both thrilling and stable.

Stocks for Growth: Stocks are like the high-flying trapeze artists of your portfolio. They soar through the air with grace and daring, aiming for the highest heights. These performers offer the potential for significant growth and returns over time, capturing the audience's imagination with their breathtaking stunts. However, with high rewards come higher risks. Just as trapeze artists sometimes miss their catches, stocks can experience volatility and sudden drops. Yet, their ability to achieve remarkable gains makes them an exciting and essential part of your investment ensemble.

Bonds for Balance: Bonds are your portfolio's safety nets. Imagine them as the sturdy nets that catch the trapeze artists if they fall. These investments offer more stable returns, providing a sense of security and balance to your portfolio. Bonds are dependable and less prone to the dramatic ups and downs of stocks. They cushion the fall during turbulent times, ensuring that your investment performance remains steady. With bonds in place, you can enjoy the thrill of the trapeze without constantly worrying about the risks.

Alternatives for Spice: Now, think of real estate, commodities, and funds like ETFs as the exotic acts that add an extra layer of excitement and variety to the show. These performers bring unique skills and flavors to the circus, diversifying the entertainment and keeping the audience engaged. Alternatives can provide additional avenues for growth and stability, each reacting differently to market conditions. Real estate might offer steady rental income, commodities can hedge against inflation, and ETFs allow you to invest in a broad range of assets with ease. Together, these investments spice up your portfolio, spreading out the risk and enhancing potential returns.

By incorporating stocks, bonds, and alternatives into your portfolio, you create a balanced and diversified investment performance. Each element complements the others, ensuring that your overall portfolio can handle the market's ups and downs while striving for growth. Just as a circus needs a mix of acts to keep the audience entertained and secure, your portfolio benefits from a blend of investments to achieve financial success.

Think of this mix as the recipe for a harmonious and resilient investment strategy. By thoughtfully combining high-risk, high-reward stocks with the stability of bonds and the unique benefits of alternatives, you craft a portfolio that is well-equipped to navigate the complexities of the financial markets. This diversified approach helps you capture growth opportunities, maintain balance, and add an extra layer of protection against unexpected market shifts.

3: Implementing Your Strategy

Once you've assessed your ingredients and chosen your mix, it's time to put your investment plan into action. Implementing your strategy effectively is crucial to building and maintaining a balanced and diversified portfolio. Here's how to get started:

Start Small: You don't need a fortune to start investing. Think of this step as planting the first seeds in your financial garden. Investing in mutual funds or ETFs (Exchange-Traded Funds) can be an excellent way to begin. These funds pool money from many investors to buy a diversified mix of stocks, bonds, or other assets.

This means you get the benefit of a diversified portfolio even with a small initial investment. It's like buying a ticket to a buffet where you get to taste a little bit of everything, ensuring that no single bad dish (or investment) ruins your meal.

Use Robo-Advisors and Financial Advisors: Technology has made investing more accessible than ever. Robo-advisors are online platforms that use algorithms to create and manage a diversified portfolio for you. Based on your risk tolerance and goals, these tools automatically adjust your investments to keep them aligned with your strategy. They're like your personal sous-chef, handling the tedious work so you can focus on the bigger picture.

However, if you prefer a more personal touch, consider working with a financial advisor. These professionals offer tailored advice and can help you navigate complex financial decisions. They act like master chefs, providing expertise and guidance to enhance your investment strategy. Whether you choose a robo-advisor, a financial advisor, or a combination of both, having professional assistance can make a significant difference in achieving your financial goals.

Regular Reviews: Just as you might adjust your seating position at the buffet to get the best access to your favorite dishes, it's essential to regularly review and adjust your portfolio. The financial markets are dynamic, and your personal circumstances and goals may change over time. Regularly reviewing your portfolio ensures it stays in line with your objectives and risk tolerance. This could involve rebalancing your investments to maintain your desired mix of stocks, bonds, and alternatives. Think of it as fine-tuning your garden—pruning, watering, and sometimes planting new seeds to keep it flourishing.

Regular reviews are crucial because they help you stay proactive rather than reactive. By periodically checking in on your investments, you can make timely adjustments and avoid potential pitfalls. It's like keeping an eye on your cooking—making sure nothing burns or gets overcooked, ensuring the final dish is as perfect as possible.

Implementing your investment strategy is an ongoing process that requires attention and care. Starting small, leveraging professional advice, and maintaining regular reviews will help you build a robust and resilient portfolio. Each step you take brings you closer to achieving your financial goals, making the journey rewarding and enjoyable.

Step 4: Keep Your Costs in Check
When it comes to investing, keeping your costs in check is crucial. Just as every transaction at a buffet can add up, so too can the fees associated with investing. Being mindful of these costs ensures that more of your money is working for you, rather than being spent on unnecessary expenses.

Remember, every investment transaction can come with fees. These fees might include management fees, transaction costs, or expense ratios, all of which can eat into your returns over time. Think of it as avoiding those extra charges for premium dishes at a buffet. While they might seem small individually, they can add up quickly and take a significant bite out of your budget.

Choosing low-cost index funds or ETFs (Exchange-Traded Funds) can help keep more of your money invested rather than spent on fees. Index funds track a specific market index, like the S&P 500, and typically have lower management fees because they are passively managed. ETFs, which also track various indices or sectors, offer similar benefits and can be bought and sold like stocks. Both options provide broad market exposure and diversification at a lower cost. It's like opting for high-quality, affordable dishes at the buffet, ensuring you get the best value for your money.

Picture this step as budgeting for a shopping spree. You want to get the most bang for your buck without blowing your budget on expensive designer items. Just as you'd look for sales or discounts to make your money go further, choosing low-cost investment options helps you maximize your returns. Opting for quality but affordable choices ensures you get everything you need without unnecessary splurges.

Additionally, be aware of other potential costs like account maintenance fees or advisory fees if you're using a financial advisor. These fees can vary widely, so it's essential to understand what you're being charged and why. By comparing different investment options and their associated costs, you can make more informed decisions that align with your financial goals.

Keeping your costs in check also involves being strategic about how often you trade. Frequent trading can incur higher transaction costs, which can quickly add up. Instead, adopting a long-term investment approach can help minimize these costs while allowing your investments to grow. It's like planning your shopping trips carefully to avoid unnecessary trips and expenses.

In summary, managing investment costs effectively is like being a savvy shopper. By choosing low-cost funds, being aware of all potential fees, and trading strategically, you ensure that more of your money stays invested and working towards your financial goals. This approach helps you build a stronger, more cost-efficient portfolio, paving the way for a successful and rewarding investment journey.

The Joy Of Diversification: A Party In Your Portfolio

Now that you've spread your investments across various assets, you've not only minimized your risk but also set the stage for a potentially rewarding investment journey. With each asset reacting differently to market changes, you're better positioned to weather financial storms.
Imagine you're throwing a big, exciting party. You wouldn't

just have one type of music playing all night, right? The same principle applies to investing. Diversifying your investments is like setting up a party with a variety of entertainment options to keep everyone engaged and happy. Now that you've spread your investments across various assets, you've not only minimized your risk but also set the stage for a potentially rewarding investment journey. With each asset reacting differently to market changes, you're better positioned to weather financial storms.

Think of diversification as your portfolio's party planning committee. With a well-chosen mix, there's always something celebrating gains, making the overall experience more enjoyable and less stressful. It's like having both a DJ and a live band at your party—if one doesn't get the guests dancing, the other surely will. This blend ensures that no matter what happens, the party keeps going strong, and everyone has a great time.

Diversification turns your investment journey into a lively, well-orchestrated celebration. Each asset class brings its own rhythm, ensuring there's never a dull moment. Whether markets are up or down, you've got a dynamic ensemble keeping the festivities alive and your financial goals on track.

By spreading your investments across different types of assets —such as stocks, bonds, and alternatives like real estate or commodities—you create a financial symphony. Stocks might be the upbeat pop songs, bringing energy and potential for high returns. Bonds are the slow, soothing ballads, providing stability and balance. Alternatives, like real estate and commodities, add that unexpected twist, like a surprise guest performer who brings something unique to the party.

This mix means that if one type of investment isn't performing well, others might be. For instance, during a stock market downturn, bonds might hold steady or even gain value, cushioning the impact on your overall portfolio. Similarly, if the bond market is sluggish, stocks or alternative investments could be thriving. This interplay of different assets helps ensure that your portfolio remains resilient and adaptable, much like a well-planned party that can handle any surprises.

Diversification also reduces the stress of trying to predict which single investment will outperform the others. Instead of putting all your eggs in one basket and hoping for the best, you're spreading them out across multiple baskets. This strategy enhances your chances of achieving consistent returns over time, without the anxiety of betting everything on one potential winner.

In essence, diversification allows you to enjoy the best of all worlds. It's like having a party where every guest's favorite music is played, and there's always someone on the dance floor. This balanced approach not only minimizes risk but also maximizes the potential for rewards, making your investment journey smoother and more enjoyable.

So, think of your diversified portfolio as a grand celebration, with each asset class playing its part in creating a harmonious and vibrant financial experience. No matter what market conditions arise, you've got a well-rounded team ready to keep the festivities alive and your financial goals on track. Cheers to the joy of diversification!

Diversification: Not Just Smart, But Essential

By now, you should see diversification not just as a strategy but as an essential part of your investing journey. It's about making smart choices, balancing your risks, and enjoying a variety of financial flavors. And who doesn't like a well-balanced meal at a finance buffet?

So, as you go forth and diversify, remember: a well-mixed portfolio brings peace of mind, potential for growth, and a way to enjoy the investment journey, no matter what the market throws at you. Let's keep the party in your portfolio going strong!

CHAPTER 6: NAVIGATING THE INVESTMENT HIGHWAY

Dollar-Cost Averaging and the Magic of Compound Interest

Welcome to the School of Smart Spending. Buckle up, dear reader! We're about to take a ride down the Investment Highway, and I promise, it's more exciting than any road trip you've been on (and yes, even that one with the all-you-can-eat pancake stops). In this chapter, we're going to master two techniques that can turn even the greenest of investors into savvy financial navigators: Dollar-Cost Averaging and the power of Compound Interest.

Part 1: Dollar-Cost Averaging – The Tortoise's Approach to Winning the Race

Let's kick things off with Dollar-Cost Averaging (DCA), a strategy that's as steady as a tortoise and just as wise. But what is it exactly?

Dollar-Cost Averaging Explained:

Imagine you're at an amusement park, and there's that one ride you just can't miss. But the line is long, and the ticket prices fluctuate like a popcorn machine on overdrive. One minute it's cheap, the next it's pricey. Instead of trying to game the system and wait for the lowest price (which could mean missing out entirely), you buy a ticket at regular intervals, no matter the cost. Over time, your average ticket price levels out, and you ride without blowing your budget.

That's Dollar-Cost Averaging. You invest a fixed amount into a particular stock or fund at regular intervals (say, monthly), regardless of the share price at the time of purchase. Sometimes you'll buy when prices are high, other times when they're low, but over time, your investment should average out to a lower overall cost per share.

Why Use Dollar-Cost Averaging?

- **Simplicity:** No need to time the market or make complicated predictions. It's as easy as setting a reminder on your phone to buy your tickets at regular intervals.
- **Consistency:** It helps you stay committed to your investment plan. Just like consistently visiting the amusement park, you're continuously participating in the market.
- **Reduces Risk:** By spreading the purchase price over time, you reduce the risk of investing a large amount at the wrong time. It's like spreading out your thrill rides throughout the day, rather than risking it all on one unpredictable coaster.

Using Dollar-Cost Averaging is like adopting the mindset of the wise tortoise from Aesop's fable, "The Tortoise and the Hare." Instead of rushing to invest a lump sum all at once, you're methodically investing smaller amounts over time. This steady, disciplined approach helps you avoid the pitfalls of market volatility.

Imagine the market as a bustling farmers' market. The prices of fresh produce vary week by week. If you commit to buying your veggies every Saturday, sometimes you'll snag a deal, and other times you might pay a bit more. Over time, however, your average cost will be more reasonable than if you tried to guess the best day to shop each week.

The beauty of Dollar-Cost Averaging is that it takes the guesswork out of investing. You don't have to be a market expert or spend hours analyzing trends. You just stick to your plan, rain or shine. This consistency not only builds a habit of regular investing but also reduces the emotional rollercoaster that comes with trying to time the market.

So, as we embark on this Investment Highway, remember the tortoise's wisdom: slow and steady wins the race. By embracing Dollar-Cost Averaging, you set the stage for a smoother, less stressful investment journey. Stay tuned, because next up, we're diving into the magical world of Compound Interest, where your money works harder than you ever imagined.

Part 2: The Power Of Compound Interest – The Sorcery Of Spontaneous Money Multiplication

Now, let's talk about a concept so magical, it could make Hogwarts look like a community college: Compound Interest. It's the secret sauce that makes the financial world spin, and once you understand it, you'll want to start investing faster than you can say "Abracadabra!"

Understanding Compound Interest:
Imagine planting a tree. This isn't just any tree; it's a Money Tree. The seeds are the initial dollars you invest. Over time, not only does the tree grow, producing more money fruits, but those fruits

drop and grow new trees of their own. As years pass, you don't just have one tree, but an entire orchard, all sprouting from your initial investment.

That's compound interest — your money makes money, then that money makes more money, and so on. It's the financial version of a family reunion where everyone brings a friend, and those friends bring more friends, and before you know it, you need to rent out a park for the annual barbecue.

How to Harness the Power of Compound Interest:

1. Start Early: The sooner you plant your Money Tree, the more time it has to grow. Think of this as the golden rule of compound interest. Time is your greatest ally here. The earlier you start investing, the more time your money has to grow and multiply. Even small amounts can grow significantly over a long period. Imagine planting an acorn today and watching it grow into a towering oak tree over the decades.

2. Reinvest Your Earnings: Let the fruits of your investment fall back into the soil. In other words, reinvest your dividends and interest. When your investments pay you returns, don't cash out. Instead, reinvest those returns to buy more shares or units. This reinvestment is like planting new seeds from your money fruits, leading to more trees and, consequently, more fruits in the future. It's a cycle that keeps on giving, amplifying your wealth over time.

3. Stay Committed: Even when the market seems dry, keep watering your investment. Consistency is key. Just like a gardener tends to their plants regularly, you need to keep investing regularly, regardless of market conditions. Market downturns might feel like a drought, but sticking with your investment plan through thick and thin ensures that your Money Tree continues to grow. Over time, these consistent contributions will compound, leading to substantial growth.

To visualize the magic of compound interest, picture a snowball rolling down a hill. As it rolls, it picks up more snow, growing larger and larger. By the time it reaches the bottom, it's a massive snow boulder. Your investments work similarly: they start small but grow exponentially as they pick up more interest over time.

Albert Einstein reportedly called compound interest the "eighth wonder of the world." He said, "He who understands it, earns it; he who doesn't, pays it." This means that by understanding and leveraging compound interest, you can significantly grow your wealth. On the flip side, ignoring it (such as through high-interest debt) can lead to financial difficulties.

So, as we continue our journey down the Investment Highway, remember that compound interest is your magical, money-multiplying companion. It's the spell that turns your initial investment into a flourishing financial forest. Embrace its power by starting early, reinvesting your earnings, and staying committed to your investment plan. With time and patience, you'll see the enchanting results unfold, transforming your financial future in ways you never imagined. Get ready to watch your wealth grow as if by magic!

Combining Dca And Compound Interest – A Match Made In Financial Heaven

Now that you know these two strategies, let's talk about how they can work together. By using Dollar-Cost Averaging (DCA), you're regularly adding seeds to your orchard, and with compound interest, each of those seeds has the potential to grow exponentially.

A Real-Life Example:

Imagine this: You're planning a cross-country road trip. Every month, you diligently save $100 for your trip. Regardless of whether gas prices soar or fall, you keep saving consistently. This disciplined approach is your Dollar-Cost Averaging. Now, suppose you deposit this monthly $100 into a high-yield savings account or a mutual fund. As you accumulate more money, you earn interest on your savings, and you reinvest that interest to earn even more. This is the magic of compound interest.

Fast forward 20, 30, or even 40 years. Thanks to your consistent savings and the power of compound interest, your modest monthly contributions have grown into a substantial travel fund. This combination of DCA and compound interest is like having a reliable car and a never-ending supply of fuel. Your journey becomes smoother, and your destination more attainable.

Think back to when you first learned to ride a bike. Initially, you practiced a little every day, pedaling down the street, sometimes wobbling but always pushing forward. That's Dollar-Cost Averaging: small, consistent efforts over time. As you got better, you started to explore further, feeling the wind in your hair and the thrill of new adventures. This growing confidence and the distance you covered represent compound interest.

Now, combine these experiences. Imagine you continue riding your bike every day, exploring new places, and becoming more skilled. Over the years, you've mapped out countless routes, discovered hidden gems, and maybe even inspired others to join you. The more you ride, the more you gain—not just in distance, but in experiences and memories. This is the synergy of DCA and compound interest: steady, consistent effort coupled with the exponential growth of your investment.

The Road Ahead: Embracing Your New Strategies

Armed with these strategies, you're now ready to drive down the Investment Highway with confidence. Remember, investing isn't just about making money; it's about making smart choices that align with your financial goals and lifestyle. With DCA and compound interest in your toolkit, you have what you need to build wealth slowly, surely, and magically.

Picture this journey as planning and embarking on that epic road trip. Each month's investment is like planning your next stop, booking accommodations, and mapping out your route. Over time, your investments grow, your trip becomes richer, and your adventures more memorable.

So, dear investor, as we close this chapter, remember that the journey of a thousand miles begins with a single step—or in your case, a single investment. Just as every mile traveled brings you closer to your destination, every dollar invested brings you closer to your financial dreams. Stay committed, keep investing, and watch your financial orchard flourish into a bountiful harvest. Happy investing, and enjoy the ride!

CHAPTER 7: OOPS! AVOIDING COMMON INVESTING BLUNDERS

Welcome to the No-Facepalm Zone

Investing can be as thrilling as a rollercoaster ride. The ups and downs, the twists and turns—it's all part of the excitement. But just like rollercoasters, there are safety rules to follow unless you want to end up with your pockets inside out. In this chapter, we're diving into some of the goofiest goofs and the most avoidable uh-ohs of the investing world. Strap in, and let's keep those investments facepalm-free!

Picture this: You're at the entrance of the world's biggest amusement park. The rides are calling your name, and the anticipation is electric. But before you dash off to the nearest rollercoaster, the park staff hands you a map and a list of safety rules. These guidelines aren't there to spoil your fun—they're there to make sure you enjoy the thrills without any spills.

The investing world is much the same. It's a landscape full of opportunities, but also potential pitfalls. By understanding and avoiding common mistakes, you can make the most of your investment journey without the dreaded facepalm moments.

So, dear reader, as we buckle up for this journey, let's commit to making smart, informed decisions. With a bit of knowledge and a steady approach, you can enjoy the exhilarating ride of investing without the embarrassing mishaps. Welcome to the No-Facepalm Zone—let's keep those investments smooth and those pockets right-side out!

Emotional Investing: When Your Heart Takes Over Your Portfolio

The Heart Wants What It Wants—But It Shouldn't Handle Your Investments

Have you ever bought a stock because it felt like it was just *calling* to you? Or maybe you held onto an investment because you loved the company's logo? That, my friend, is emotional investing, and it's about as risky as texting your ex at 2 AM.

Emotional investing is when you make financial decisions based on how you *feel* rather than what the numbers and trends suggest. It's like eating cake for dinner just because it's been a rough day. Feels great at the moment, not so great when your energy crashes.

Symptoms of Emotional Investing:

- **Panic Selling:** The market dips, and you sell everything at a loss because, well, panic!
- **Revenge Trading:** Trying to win back what you lost on bad investments by making even riskier bets.
- **Falling in Love:** Clinging to a losing stock because you believe in the company, despite all signs pointing south.

Prescription: Keep Your Cool

- **Have a Plan**: Set clear, emotion-free goals for each investment.
- **Stay Informed:** Make decisions based on research, not gut feelings.
- **Diversify:** Spread out your investments to reduce the risk of

emotional attachment to any single one.

Timing The Market: The Investor's Fool's Errand

Trying to Be a Time Traveler in the Stock Market

Timing the market is like trying to jump onto a moving train based on a guess when it might slow down. It sounds cool and daring, but it's more likely to end with you sprawled on the platform. Market timing involves trying to predict the best times to buy low and sell high, and even the pros get it wrong.

Why Market Timing Misses the Mark:

- **It's Crystal Ball Stuff:** No one really knows what the market will do tomorrow. Economists can guess, but they're often as clueless as the rest of us.
- **Missed Opportunities:** While you wait for the "perfect moment" to invest, you might miss out on steady gains.
- **Extra Costs:** Frequent buying and selling can lead to higher transaction fees and taxes.

Better Strategy: Ride It Out

- **Regular Investing:** Use dollar-cost averaging to invest a consistent amount regularly. It's less stressful than trying to time your entry and exit.
- **Long-Term Focus:** Keep your eyes on the horizon, not on the waves right in front of you.
- Patience Pays: The market tends to grow over time, even if it has ups and downs along the way.

Keeping Your Investments On The Logic Train

By now, you've probably realized that the key to avoiding these common investing mistakes is to keep your cool and stick to a plan. Emotional investing and trying to time the market are like junk food for your portfolio—tempting but unhealthy.

Here's a quick recap to keep your investments healthy and your regrets minimal:

- **Emotions Check:** Treat your investments like a science experiment. Observe, hypothesize, test, and conclude—leave feelings out of it.
- **No Crystal Balling:** Accept that you can't predict the market. Invest regularly and focus on the long haul.
- **Educate Yourself:** The more you know, the less likely you are to make decisions on a whim.

Investing is a marathon, not a sprint. By avoiding these common mistakes, you're setting yourself up for a less stressful and potentially more profitable journey. So keep your head clear, your goals in sight, and your investments diversified. Happy investing, and here's to making all your financial dreams come true without the facepalms!

CHAPTER 8: KEEPING YOUR INVESTMENTS FIT AND FAB: MONITORING AND KNOWING WHEN TO SAY GOODBYE

Welcome to the Investment Gym!

Just like you wouldn't expect to get fit by visiting the gym once and never going back, you can't expect your investments to thrive without a little regular check-up and maintenance. This chapter is all about keeping your investments healthy, robust, and working hard for you. Grab your financial fitness tracker—it's time to tone your portfolio!

Step 1: Monitoring Your Portfolio – The Art Of Financial Stalking

Why Monitor?

Imagine your investments are like houseplants. You can't just water them once and expect them to flourish forever. They need consistent care—sunlight, water, maybe a little chat here and there (plants love a good pep talk). Monitoring your portfolio ensures your investments are still aligned with your financial goals and are not wilting under economic pressure.

Think of your portfolio as a vibrant garden. Each investment is a different plant, requiring specific attention and care. Some need more sunlight (growth stocks), while others thrive in the shade (bonds). By regularly checking in on your garden, you ensure that every plant gets what it needs to thrive, creating a lush, diverse, and flourishing landscape.

How to Monitor Like a Pro:

- **Set a Schedule:** Choose a regular interval to check on your investments. It could be monthly, quarterly, or semi-annually, depending on how hands-on you want to be. Think of this as setting reminders to water your plants or give them a little extra sunlight. Consistency is key to ensuring your garden stays healthy.

- **Use Tools:** Leverage apps and platforms that help track your investments. Many brokers offer tools that let you see the performance of your assets in real-time, much like a fitness tracker shows you how many steps you've taken. These tools can provide valuable insights, such as growth trends, dividend payouts, and market comparisons, helping you make informed decisions.

- **Look at Performance vs. Goals:** Are your investments doing what you expected them to do? If you bought stocks hoping for growth, are they growing? If you invested in bonds for steady income, is the income coming in? This is like checking if your sunflowers are towering over the garden or if your herb garden is providing a steady supply of fresh ingredients. Matching performance with expectations helps you understand whether your investment strategy is on track.

-**Check the Economic Weather:** Economic conditions can affect your investments. Keeping an eye on market trends, interest rate changes, and economic news can help you understand why your investments are performing the way they are. It's like checking the weather forecast to decide whether to cover your plants during a storm or give them extra water during a heatwave. Being aware of the economic climate helps you anticipate and react to changes that might impact your portfolio.

Monitoring your portfolio is akin to being a vigilant gardener. By staying attentive and proactive, you can spot issues early and make adjustments to keep your investments thriving. This might involve pruning underperforming assets, replanting into more fertile ground (diversifying), or adding new plants (investments) to enhance your garden's overall health.

Why This Matters:
Regular monitoring ensures that your financial garden remains aligned with your goals and adaptable to changing conditions. It helps you avoid unpleasant surprises and gives you the confidence to make informed decisions. Whether you're saving for retirement, a dream home, or a grand adventure, keeping a close eye on your investments ensures they continue to grow and support your aspirations.

So, dear investor, embrace the art of financial stalking. Set your schedule, use the right tools, and stay informed about the economic weather. Your portfolio will thank you with steady growth and bountiful returns, just like a well-tended garden rewards you with a beautiful, thriving oasis.

Step 2: Rebalancing – Keeping Your Financial Diet Balanced

What is Rebalancing?

Back to our diet analogy: If you're eating nothing but carrots, you're going to turn orange. Similarly, if too much of your money is tied up in one type of investment, your portfolio might get a bit... unbalanced. Rebalancing is the process of realigning the weight of each asset in your portfolio to maintain your desired level of asset allocation.

Think of your portfolio as a well-balanced diet. Just as your body needs a mix of proteins, carbohydrates, and fats to stay healthy, your investments need a mix of assets like stocks, bonds, and alternatives to stay robust and resilient. Over time, some assets will grow faster than others, causing your once-balanced diet to become skewed—too much of one thing and not enough of another. Rebalancing is like adjusting your diet to ensure you're getting the right nutrients in the right proportions.

How to Rebalance Without Tipping Over:

- **Determine Your Ideal Asset Allocation:** This is based on your risk tolerance, investment goals, and time horizon. It might be something like 60% stocks and 40% bonds. Your ideal allocation is like your personalized meal plan, designed to meet your unique nutritional needs and lifestyle. For instance, if you're aiming for growth and can handle more risk, your plan might include a higher percentage of stocks. If you're closer to retirement and prefer stability, you might favor bonds.

- **Analyze Your Current Portfolio:** How has your asset allocation shifted over time? Maybe your stocks did really well, and now they make up 70% of your portfolio. This is like checking in with your diet after a few months and realizing you've been indulging in too many carbs and not enough veggies. Regular analysis helps you understand where your portfolio is off balance and where adjustments are needed.

- **Make Adjustments:** Sell off some of what you have too much of and buy more of what you have too little. This might mean selling some stocks and buying more bonds to get back to your 60/40 split. Rebalancing is like adjusting your meals to ensure you're getting the right mix of nutrients. If you've been eating too many sweets, you cut back and add more greens to your plate. Similarly, if your stocks have surged and now dominate your portfolio, you sell a portion and reinvest in bonds or other underrepresented assets.

Why Rebalancing Matters:
Rebalancing keeps your portfolio aligned with your risk tolerance and investment goals. Just as a balanced diet promotes overall health, a balanced portfolio ensures that your investments remain diversified and resilient against market fluctuations. Without rebalancing, your portfolio could become overly concentrated in one asset class, increasing your risk exposure. It's like ignoring your diet until all you're left with is a plate full of sweets—tempting but unhealthy in the long run.

When to Rebalance:

- **Regular Intervals:** Many investors choose to rebalance on a set schedule, such as annually or semi-annually. It's like having a regular health check-up to ensure everything is on track.
- **Threshold Trigger:** Another approach is to rebalance whenever your asset allocation deviates from your target by a certain percentage, say 5%. This is akin to adjusting your diet whenever you notice significant weight changes or health issues.

Rebalancing ensures that you're not taking on more risk than you intended and that your investments are working towards your goals. It's a crucial step in maintaining a healthy, diversified portfolio. By regularly rebalancing, you're keeping your financial diet in check, ensuring that you have the right mix of assets to support your financial health and growth.

So, as you continue your investment journey, remember to monitor and rebalance your portfolio. This disciplined approach will help you navigate market changes and keep your investments aligned with your goals. Just like maintaining a balanced diet, regular rebalancing is key to long-term financial well-being. Step 3: Knowing When to Cash Out – Timing Your Financial Farewells

Why It's Hard To Say Goodbye

Deciding when to sell an investment is like breaking up with someone you've been with for a long time. It's not easy, and emotions can get in the way. But just like in relationships, not all investments are meant to be forever. Knowing when to let go is crucial.

Signs It's Time to Say Goodbye:

- **Goal Achievement:** If you invested to pay for a child's college, and now they're packing their bags for freshman year, it might be time to cash out. This is like completing a marathon. You've trained hard, run the race, and now it's time to cross the finish line and celebrate your achievement.

- **Fundamental Changes:** If the fundamentals of a company you've invested in have deteriorated (think scandal, massive debt, loss of a major customer), it might be time to reconsider your position. This is similar to realizing a long-term partner has changed in ways that no longer align with your values or goals.

- **Overvaluation:** If your research shows that an asset is significantly overvalued compared to its historical norms and you believe it can't sustain those levels, consider selling. It's like deciding to sell your house when the market is at its peak. You recognize that the current high prices aren't sustainable and it's a smart time to cash out.

- **Life Changes:** Changes in your personal life—retirement, buying a house, or a change in your risk tolerance—might necessitate a change in your investment strategy. This is akin to adapting your exercise routine as you age or after an injury. Your needs and capacities change, and so should your approach.

Keeping It All Together – Your Investment Fitness Plan

Monitoring, rebalancing, and knowing when to cash out are all integral parts of maintaining and growing your investment. Think of yourself as the coach of your own financial fitness center. It's your job to make sure every financial muscle is in top form and that your overall investment health is robust.

- **Monitoring:** Regularly check in on your investments to ensure they're performing as expected. This is like tracking your workouts and progress in a fitness journal. Keeping tabs on your performance helps you stay on course and make necessary adjustments.

- **Rebalancing:** Periodically adjust your portfolio to maintain your desired asset allocation. This is similar to mixing up your workout routine to target different muscle groups and avoid imbalances. Rebalancing keeps your portfolio aligned with your goals and risk tolerance.

- **Knowing When to Cash Out:** Recognize the signs that it's time to sell an investment. This is like knowing when to take a rest day or switch up your exercise regimen to prevent burnout and injury. Selling at the right time ensures that you lock in gains and adjust your strategy as needed.

As you become more comfortable with these practices, they'll become second nature, like a daily workout for your wallet. Keep your eyes on the prize, stay informed, and remember: the goal is not just to play the game but to win it.

Staying Motivated:

Think of your financial journey as a long-term fitness plan. Just as you stay hydrated, eat well, and exercise regularly to keep your body in peak condition, you should stay informed, make smart decisions, and regularly review your investments to keep your portfolio healthy.

So keep those financial sneakers laced up, stay hydrated with fresh market insights, and keep moving forward. Here's to your continued financial health and growing wealth!

By embracing these practices, you ensure that your investment strategy remains dynamic, resilient, and aligned with your financial goals. Treat your portfolio like an athlete, always striving for peak performance through careful monitoring, regular adjustments, and timely decisions. Happy investing! Conclusion: The Never-Ending Investment Journey

Keep Climbing: The Lifelong Learning Ladder

Congratulations, dear investor! You've made it to the end of this wild, whirlwind tour of the investment world. But before you put this book on your shelf and call it a day, remember: the realm of investing is always evolving, just like your favorite long-running TV show. There's always a new episode, and if you stop watching, you might miss some critical twists and turns!

Continuing Your Investment Education

Investing isn't a "set it and forget it" crockpot recipe; it's more like tending to a sourdough starter. It's a living, breathing world where new information, technologies, and strategies pop up like mushrooms after rain. Staying informed and continuing your investment education is crucial. Here's how to keep your knowledge fresh:

- **Read Widely and Often:** Stay updated with financial news, blogs, podcasts, and books. The more you know, the better equipped you'll be to make informed decisions. Think of it as keeping your investment garden well-watered and free of weeds. The more you read, the more you grow. Read a variety of sources to get diverse perspectives—financial journals for in-depth analysis, blogs for personal insights, podcasts for expert interviews, and books for comprehensive knowledge. Make it a habit to consume new content regularly, turning it into a daily or weekly ritual.

- **Courses and Workshops:** Consider enrolling in online courses or local workshops. This is like going to the gym for your brain! Just as regular exercise keeps your body fit, continuous learning keeps your financial acumen sharp. Look for courses that cover topics you're interested in or areas where you feel less confident. Workshops provide hands-on experience and the opportunity to ask questions and interact with instructors and peers. Websites like Coursera, Udemy, and local community colleges offer a plethora of options to suit different schedules and learning preferences.

- **Networking:** Join investment clubs or online communities. Sharing experiences and strategies with fellow investors can provide new insights and keep you motivated. It's like having a workout buddy who pushes you to reach your goals and celebrates your milestones with you. Networking allows you to exchange ideas, learn from others' mistakes and successes, and stay updated on market trends. Consider attending financial seminars, webinars, or local investment meetups. Online forums and social media groups dedicated to investing can also be valuable resources.

Staying Motivated: The Marathon, Not The Sprint

Investing is not for the sprinters who seek immediate gratification. It's a marathon, possibly one that lasts your entire life. Here's why staying motivated and maintaining your stamina is key:

- **The Power of Persistence:** Rome wasn't built in a day, and similarly, significant investment returns aren't made overnight. It takes time for your investments to mature and for compound interest to work its magic. Think of each investment as a brick in the grand structure of your financial future. Keep adding bricks consistently, and over time, you'll see your wealth grow. Persistence means sticking to your investment plan even during tough times, trusting that your strategy will pay off in the long run.

- **Patience Is Your Ally:** The market will test your patience with its ups and downs. Staying the course, rather than reacting to short-term volatility, often yields the best results. It's like running a marathon where the terrain changes from smooth to rocky. Keeping a steady pace ensures you don't burn out before reaching the finish line. Patience involves resisting the urge to make hasty decisions based on market noise. Instead, focus on your long-term goals and the big picture, understanding that fluctuations are part of the journey.

- **Celebrate Small Victories:** Did your stock portfolio go up this year? Did you finally understand what an ETF is? Celebrate these wins; they're signs of progress! Just as marathon runners celebrate each mile marker, recognizing your achievements keeps you motivated and focused. Celebrating small victories reinforces positive behavior and helps maintain momentum. It could be as simple as treating yourself to a nice dinner or taking a day off to relax and reflect on your accomplishments.

Your Investment Journey Continues

As you continue to climb the lifelong learning ladder, remember that investing is a journey, not a destination. There will always be new challenges, opportunities, and lessons to learn. Embrace this journey with curiosity and enthusiasm.

- **Stay Curious:** Never stop asking questions or seeking new knowledge. The more curious you are, the more you'll discover about the ever-changing world of investing. Curiosity drives you to explore new markets, understand emerging technologies, and stay ahead of trends. Approach investing with a learner's mindset, always eager to uncover new insights and improve your strategies.

- **Adapt and Evolve:** The investment landscape is always shifting. Being adaptable and open to new strategies will help you stay ahead. It's like learning new dance moves to stay in sync with the latest music trends. Adaptability means being willing to reassess and adjust your portfolio as needed. It involves staying flexible and open-minded, ready to pivot when new opportunities or challenges arise.

- **Enjoy the Ride:** Investing should be exciting and fulfilling. Relish the process of learning, growing, and building your financial future. Think of it as an adventure where every step forward brings new insights and achievements. Enjoying the ride means finding joy in the journey itself, not just the destination. Celebrate your progress, learn from your setbacks, and take pride in your ongoing growth.

So, dear investor, keep those financial sneakers laced up, stay hydrated with fresh market insights, and keep moving forward. Your journey doesn't end here—it's just beginning. Here's to your continued financial health and growing wealth! May you climb higher, learn more, and achieve all your financial dreams without the facepalms. Happy investing, and cheers to a prosperous future!

By embracing these practices, you ensure that your investment strategy remains dynamic, resilient, and aligned with your financial goals. Treat your portfolio like an athlete, always striving for peak performance through careful monitoring, regular adjustments, and timely decisions. Happy investing! Appendix: Your Investment Toolkit

No educational journey would be complete without a handy

glossary and some resources for further reading. Consider this your investment toolbox—tools that you'll come back to time and again as you continue to navigate the investment landscape.

Wrap-Up: The Adventure Continues

While this book may end, your adventure in investing is just beginning. Every chapter you read, every term you understand, and every investment you make is a step toward becoming a more confident and capable investor. Remember, the world of finance is not static; it evolves, and so should you. Keep learning, stay patient, and keep those investments growing. Here's to your ongoing journey in the exciting world of investing! Happy investing, and may your newfound knowledge empower you.

GLOSSARY

Asset Allocation: The process of deciding how to distribute your investment portfolio among different asset categories, such as stocks, bonds, and cash.

Bear Market: A period of declining stock prices, typically by 20% or more, characterized by widespread pessimism and negative investor sentiment.

Bonds: Debt securities issued by corporations, municipalities, or governments. When you buy a bond, you are lending money to the issuer in exchange for periodic interest payments and the return of the bond's face value when it matures.

Bull Market: A period of rising stock prices, typically by 20% or more, characterized by widespread optimism and positive investor sentiment.

Compound Interest: Interest calculated on the initial principal, which also includes all the accumulated interest from previous periods on a deposit or loan.

Diversification: The practice of spreading investments across various financial assets, industries, and other categories to reduce exposure to risk.

Dollar-Cost Averaging (DCA): An investment strategy where you invest a fixed amount of money at regular intervals, regardless of the price of the investment, to reduce the impact of volatility over time.

Economic Conditions: The state of the economy at a given time, including factors like employment rates, inflation, and interest rates, which can influence investment performance.

ETFs (Exchange-Traded Funds): Investment funds traded on stock exchanges, much like stocks. ETFs hold assets such as stocks, commodities, or bonds and generally operate with an arbitrage mechanism designed to keep trading close to its net asset value.

Fundamental Changes: Significant shifts in the fundamentals of a company, such as its financial health, management, or competitive position, which can affect its stock price.

Interest Rate: The amount a lender charges a borrower and is a percentage of the principal—the amount loaned. It is also the return earned on an investment or savings.

Investment Clubs: Groups of individuals who pool their money to make investments, sharing research and investment decisions.

Long-Term Focus: An investment strategy that emphasizes holding investments for an extended period, typically several years or more, to benefit from compound interest and long-term growth trends.

Market Trends: The general direction in which a market or the price of an asset is moving over a period of time, influenced by various factors including economic indicators and investor sentiment.

Mutual Funds: Investment vehicles that pool money from multiple investors to purchase a diversified portfolio of stocks, bonds, or other securities.

Overvaluation: When the price of an asset is higher than its intrinsic value or historical norms, often leading to a potential price correction.

Patience: The ability to remain invested and committed to a long-term strategy, even during periods of market volatility or downturns.

Persistence: Consistently following an investment strategy over time, regardless of short-term market conditions, to achieve long-term goals.

Portfolio: A collection of financial investments like stocks, bonds, commodities, cash, and cash equivalents, as well as their fund counterparts, such as mutual, exchange-traded, and closed funds.

Rebalancing: The process of realigning the weightings of a portfolio's assets to maintain the original or desired level of asset allocation.

Risk Tolerance: An individual's ability and willingness to endure declines in the values of investments while waiting for them to increase in value.

Stocks: Shares of ownership in a corporation. Stocks entitle the shareholder to a portion of the company's profits and assets.

Volatility: The degree of variation in the price of a financial instrument over time. High volatility means the price of the asset can change dramatically over a short period, while low volatility means the price change is more gradual.

Workshops: Educational sessions where participants engage in intensive discussion and activity on particular subjects or projects.

FURTHER RESOURCES:

These resources are just a few examples of what's available to help you continue your investment journey with confidence and knowledge. There are many other resources out there, so pick the ones that fit your learning style and mood. The key is to keep learning something new every day because **knowledge is power**. To keep your investment muscles flexed and your knowledge up to date, here are some resources to explore:

Books:
- "The Intelligent Investor" by Benjamin Graham: A must-read for understanding the value of long-term investment strategies.

- "A Random Walk Down Wall Street" by Burton Malkiel: A guide to investing and financial markets, advocating for the "random walk" hypothesis.

Websites:
- **Investopedia** (www.investopedia.com): Offers a wealth of articles, tutorials, and simulators to help you better understand investing.

- **Morningstar** (www.morningstar.com): Provides research and investment management tools; particularly known for its data on mutual funds and ETFs.

Podcasts:
- "The Indicator from Planet Money": Breaks down complex economic and financial topics into digestible parts.

- "Invest Like the Best": Explores stories and strategies from top investors.

Apps and Tools:

- **Stash** (www.stash.com): A user-friendly app for beginner investors that offers fractional shares, diversified portfolios, and educational resources.

- **Robinhood** (www.robinhood.com): A commission-free trading app that allows users to buy and sell stocks, ETFs, options, and cryptocurrencies.

- **Mint** (www.mint.com): A comprehensive budgeting app that helps users manage their finances by tracking spending, creating budgets, and providing financial insights.

- **Betterment** (www.betterment.com): A robo-advisor that offers automated investing and financial planning services based on individual goals and risk tolerance.

- **Wealthfront** (www.wealthfront.com): Another robo-advisor providing automated investment management, along with financial planning tools and a high-interest cash account.

- **Acorns** (www.acorns.com): An investment app that rounds up your everyday purchases to the nearest dollar and invests the spare change into diversified portfolios.

- **Personal Capital** (www.personalcapital.com): A budgeting app that also provides comprehensive financial planning and investment management services.

"Investing in knowledge pays the best interest." – Benjamin Franklin

www.ingramcontent.com/pod-product-compliance
Lightning Source LLC
Chambersburg PA
CBHW050110230526
45470CB00004B/1765